# ACADEMICS WRITING

## The Dynamics of Knowledge Creation

*Karin Tusting, Sharon McCulloch, Ibrar Bhatt, Mary Hamilton, and David Barton*

Routledge
Taylor & Francis Group

LONDON AND NEW YORK

First published 2019
by Routledge
2 Park Square, Milton Park, Abingdon, Oxon OX14 4RN

and by Routledge
52 Vanderbilt Avenue, New York, NY 10017

*Routledge is an imprint of the Taylor & Francis Group, an informa business*

© 2019 Karin Tusting, Sharon McCulloch, Ibrar Bhatt, Mary Hamilton and David Barton

The right of Karin Tusting, Sharon McCulloch, Ibrar Bhatt, Mary Hamilton and David Barton to be identified as authors of this work has been asserted by them in accordance with sections 77 and 78 of the Copyright, Designs and Patents Act 1988.

*British Library Cataloguing-in-Publication Data*
A catalogue record for this book is available from the British Library

*Library of Congress Cataloging-in-Publication Data*
Names: Tusting, Karin, 1973- author. | McCulloch, Sharon, author. | Bhatt, Ibrar, author. | Hamilton, Mary, 1949- author. | Barton, David, 1949- author.
Title: Academics writing : the dynamics of knowledge creation / Karin Tusting, Sharon McCulloch, Ibrar Bhatt, Mary Hamilton and David Barton.
Description: Abingdon, Oxon ; New York, NY : Routledge, 2019. | Includes bibliographical references and index.
Identifiers: LCCN 2018052442| ISBN 9780815385912 (hardback) | ISBN 9780815385905 (paperback) | ISBN 9780429197994 (e-book)
Subjects: LCSH: Academic writing.
Classification: LCC P301.5.A27 T88 2019 | DDC 808.06/6378--dc 3
LC record available at https://lccn.loc.gov/2018052442

ISBN: 978-0-815-38591-2 (hbk)
ISBN: 978-0-815-38590-5 (pbk)
ISBN: 978-0-429-19799-4 (ebk)

Typeset in Times New Roman
by Taylor & Francis Books
Printed and bound by CPI Group (UK) Ltd, Croydon, CR04YY

# CONTENTS

*List of illustrations*                                                ix
*Preface*                                                               x
*Acknowledgements*                                                    xii

1 Introduction and context for the study                               1

   *The changing university 2*
   *Research on academic writing 5*
   *Chapter by chapter outline 7*

2 Theories and methods for studying academics writing                 11

   *Framing the research: literacy studies and socio-material*
      *theory 11*
   *Implications for research design and methodology 15*
   *From principles to design 16*
   *Methodological decisions and procedures 17*
      Phase one: differently focused interviews 19
      Phase two: videography 21
      Phase three: broadening out 22
   *Data analysis 24*
   *Auto-ethnography 26*
   *Impact activities in the research sites 26*

3  Days in the lives of academics, writing                                    27

   *Clearing away the small tasks 27*
   *Meetings and multitasking 29*
   *Working from home 30*
   *Daily routines 32*
   *Finding the printer, finding the papers 33*
   *Managing email pressures 34*
   *Administrative writing and changing accountability*
    *demands 36*
   *Reactivity 37*
   *Weekly rhythm 38*
   *Autonomy in writing, support from colleagues 39*
   *Never switching off 40*
   *Control 42*
   *The importance of finishing 43*
   *Conclusion 44*

4  Academics writing in space and time                                       45

   *Introduction 45*
   *Space 46*
   *Time 52*
   *Strategies 58*
   *Conclusion 61*

5  Disciplines, genres, and writing                                          63

   *Disciplines 63*
   *Genres 65*
   *The knowledge that is valued in marketing 67*
   *The knowledge that is valued in history 71*
   *The knowledge that is valued in maths 74*
   *Conclusions 77*

6  Changing tools and technologies in academics' writing lives   79

   *Introduction and background 79*
   *Digital tools and resources 80*
   *Digital communications technologies and academics'*
    *writing practices 82*
   *What annoys you about technology at work? Affect and*
    *stance-taking 83*

*Different paths to common goals: PowerPoint as a form of
  writing 84*
*Conflicted stance: email, a blessing or a curse? 85*

7 New social media genres: Marketing the academic self     92

*Introduction: new social media genres in academia 92*
*Practices on different social media platforms 93*
*Attitudes to using social media 97*
*Advantages and possibilities of social media 98*
*Challenges associated with social media 100*
*Conclusion: professional identity and future
  implications 105*

8 Relationships and collaboration in academic writing     106

*Introduction 106*
*Sharing in research writing 107*
*Teaching collaborations 110*
*Administrative writing 113*
*Writing in service relations 117*
*Conclusions 118*

9 Learning academic writing: An ongoing process     120

*Learning at the beginning of the career 121*
*Learning from others: apprenticeship, collaboration, and
  networking 123*
*Learning from others: peer review 124*
*Learning from others: using models 125*
*Learning by doing 126*
*Learning to write for teaching 127*
*Learning writing for leadership and management 128*
*Learning meta-logistical and organisational writing 129*
*Learning social media and new technologies 131*
*Conclusion 131*

10 The futures of writing: Conclusions and implications     134

*Space and time 135*
*Managerialism 136*
*Digital technologies 137*
*Relationships, collaboration, and informal learning 138*
*Stress and pressure 139*

*Knowledge creation and different visions of writing identities 141*
*Implications: fostering a positive writing culture in academia 143*
    Implications for academics 143
    Implications for management 144
    Implications for workplace learning and professional development 145
*Future research 146*
    Extending the study 146
    Methodology 147
    International academics writing 148
*Conclusion 148*

| | |
|---|---|
| *References* | *150* |
| *Index* | *161* |

# ILLUSTRATIONS

**Figures**

2.1 Example of screen-in-screen recording                     22
2.2 Example of a coded photograph                             25
4.1 Some office spaces were very restricted                   48
4.2 Views of green space and light help this writer           50
4.3 Building works and refurbishments were common
    disruptions                                                51

**Table**

2.1 Extract from videolog                                     23

# PREFACE

In the spring of 2018, an unprecedented 14-day strike of academics and professional services staff took place in over 60 universities across the UK. The trigger for this dispute was a highly detrimental set of changes which had been proposed to the university pension scheme. But this specific issue brought to a head simmering tensions resulting from changes in higher education, which can be banded loosely together under the label of "marketisation".

Previous academic strikes had never lasted longer than a few days, and the prevailing wisdom in the union was that members would simply not stay out for longer than that. As the strike continued, however, it became clear that something quite extraordinary was happening. Pickets were reported outside university campuses of 80, 100, 150 people. Teach-outs around the country started to rebuild a vision of critical, collective learning and teaching. Several Universities were occupied by student activists, challenging the dominant account of students as neoliberal consumers. A campaign to crowdfund legal action against the pensions proposals built up £50,000 in a matter of days. Academic Twitter was filled with images of homemade placards (with slogans that were both acerbic and humorous), singing, dancing academics (and an inflatable dinosaur), showing their pleasure in engaging in collective struggle and rebuilding an almost-lost sense of collegiality.

The outcomes of the dispute – both those specific to the pensions issue, and more general shifts – are still playing out; but it is clear that during the strike and afterwards, a new energy coalesced around the conditions of work in higher education in campuses across the country. New relationships were built, new forms of collaboration were tried out, and a shared determination to resist the dominance of the competitive business model of the university was born.

This book explores the lives and experiences of UK academics in the period immediately preceding this unexpected outpouring of resistance and solidarity, through the lens of writing, one of the key activities in which academics engage in their everyday lives. It explores how academics negotiate their daily writing around the demands and constraints of the neoliberal, marketised university. It documents the requirements they face to produce many different genres of writing designed to promote universities' strategic goals and move institutions upwards in international rankings: scholarly articles and monographs, lectures, student feedback, evaluation reports of teaching and research, and multiple accounts of self. It explores the role of discipline and of institution in shaping people's experiences. It analyses relationships with management at different levels, the mediating role of heads of department, and the degree of agency individuals have in making their own writing decisions. It shows how the digital communications revolution has changed, in profound ways, what it means to be an academic. Finally, it makes proposals about how academic writing could be different, and how this could contribute to a renewed vision of the university.

Lancaster University, October 2018

# ACKNOWLEDGEMENTS

We would like to thank, first and foremost, our research participants, who were very generous with their time and engagement, and without whom this book would not have been possible. We thank also all those who participated in project events, including the various impact workshops, project conference, and writing retreat. Conversations during these events helped us to shape our ideas and develop our analyses, as well as clarifying how the work could be useful to people. Members of the project advisory group engaged with us at several key points during the development of the project and were generous in the sharing of their ideas and in their support: thank you to Paul Ashwin, Rosemary Deem, Lesley Farrell, Mary Lea, Theresa Lillis, Janice Malcolm, Rowena Murray, Greg Myers, Anna Solin, and Miriam Zukas. We would particularly like to thank Dee Daglish, our administrator, who kept everything running smoothly throughout the project. We acknowledge the support of the project funders, the Economic and Social Research Council. Finally, thank you to all of those people in our professional and personal networks who provided support as we were writing the book in many and various ways, too many to list. Academic writing is never really done alone.

# 1

# INTRODUCTION AND CONTEXT FOR THE STUDY

Academic writing practices of various kinds are central to the enterprise of higher education. It is largely through these writing practices that universities achieve their central objectives, and the success of institutions and individuals is measured against them. Writing work is at the heart of knowledge production, and traditionally the university has been a pivotal and highly valued site for this. Like other areas of work such as healthcare and manufacturing (Iedema & Scheeres, 2003), academic life is textually saturated and shaped by rapidly changing communications technologies.

Academic writing can be seen, in Scollon's terms (2002), as a "nexus of practice": a network in which a number of social practices intersect and on which all the significant forces that are currently shaping higher education converge, which forms the basis of the identities academics produce and claim through their writing actions. Close examination of how writing practices are changing, and how those changes are being managed and experienced, can therefore throw light on issues of broader significance, such as the nature of knowledge production and what it is to be an academic.

It is for this reason that we decided to take writing as our starting point and as a window through which to explore the changes that academics are living through. These include, particularly, changes in the ways universities are being run and academics are being managed, with the introduction of so-called "managerialism" in universities, and changes in the means of communication, with the ever-increasing use of digital communications technologies in research, teaching, and administration. Both of these directly shape the nature of the writing practices academics engage in, the times and places in which they write, the relationships and divisions of labour between colleagues; put in the broadest sense, the social and material resources on which they draw as they write. We explore these aspects in the pages which follow, asking how academics' writing practices are shaped by socio-material aspects of their situation; how digital communications technologies and managerialist practices shape and co-ordinate these processes; and whether there are subsequent effects on academic scholarly and professional identities, both at the level of the individual and in relation to larger groupings like disciplines and departments.

The research on which this book draws studied how knowledge is produced, shaped, and distributed through the writing practices of academic staff working across a range of disciplines and at different career stages within the contemporary English higher education system. The writing we refer to involves not just the monographs and research papers which academics produce for journals but also all the other kinds of writing academics engage in. This diversity can be divided into scholarly, pedagogic, administrative, and "impact" writing practices. We attend symmetrically (Pardoe, 2000) to the routine practices of writing for teaching and supporting students, service writing such as letters of endorsement, engaging with social media and other outward-facing promotional writing (Lupton, 2014) in the same way that we approach the writing of scholarly and research publications. We include the ubiquitous email correspondence that all academics now engage with (Jerejian, Reid, & Rees, 2013), as well as the use and maintenance of virtual learning environments (VLEs), web-based platforms used for organising teaching, learning materials, and online interactions. We also include the hidden maintenance practices of academia, the "behind the scenes" production of administrative documents that are an integral part of the knowledge production process, oiling the bureaucratic wheels that allow research projects to be carried out, the quality of student experience to be monitored, lectures to be scheduled, and online sites to function for participants across the world (Denis & Pontille, 2015). We document how all of these writing practices are changing during a period when the academy itself is changing rapidly.

This first chapter provides some background by examining how universities are changing and the current pressures on those who work in the university sector. It sets out both the general approach taken and the background research framing this study. It shows writing at the heart of academics' professional lives, with almost all the activities academics engage in centrally involving writing. It finishes with a chapter-by-chapter outline of the book.

## The changing university

Universities in England have seen considerable change over the last three decades. As a working environment, the academy has been reconfigured through increasing use of digital resources, new forms of funding, governance and accountability, and internationalization (Barnett, 2000; Robertson, 2014). We argue in this book that transformations in the higher education workplace are associated with changes in the work, responsibilities, and identities of academics (Gornall, Cook, Daunton, Salisbury, & Thomas, 2013), which can be tracked through their writing practices. It has also been argued that the very nature of academic knowledge is changing, challenging the traditional boundaries of expertise and disciplines (Deem, Hillyard, & Reed, 2007).

Several interconnected processes can be identified that currently impact on academics' work and their identities. First, higher education is now an increasingly significant global industry, competing within an international knowledge-based economy (Sum & Jessop, 2013; Radice, 2013). Within England, an expansion of higher education has seen both an increase in the overall numbers of students, and a wider diversity of students at university level. Higher education is changing from an elite to a mass system as a result of widening participation policies. International student numbers have increased and many universities now have international campuses functioning in a range of host countries (Wilkins & Huisman, 2012). There is increased staff mobility and exchange of expertise through international research projects. Traditionally privileged forms of knowledge and authority are challenged. New, competing versions of "knowledge" emerge, involving new producers and audiences, with some arguing that knowledge itself is emerging as a new form of capital (Olssen & Peters, 2005).

In England, state funding of universities has been reduced, and fees paid by individual students have become a main source of support. Students are thereby transformed into "consumers" and the teaching and research work of academics starts to be treated as a commodity to be exchanged in a competitive international marketplace (Morrish, 2018). Universities are increasingly shaped by neoliberal corporate practices: institutions are branded, marketed, and ranked in competition with one another (see Mautner, 2005, 2010; Mayr, 2008; Holborow, 2013). Many texts are produced which are designed to "sell" the university: glossy prospectuses, highly professional institutional websites. Efficiency and monetary return on individual academic labour is valued highly, replacing traditional values of public service and intellectual curiosity.

One significant effect of this corporatisation of higher education is the introduction of new systems of accountability and monitoring of professional work which have been put in place to manage academics' practices and performance (Ainsworth, Grant, & Iedema, 2009; Strathern, 2000; Shepherd, 2018). Such changes in managerial practices significantly impact on academic identity and create a situation where the forms of knowledge which are privileged are changing. They challenge long-standing traditions of professional autonomy and creativity (Tight, 2000) and the status of the academic as a public intellectual (Burawoy, 2005). There is a shift from seeing knowledge as a public good to viewing knowledge as a commodity to be sold on the market. There is less security of employment for both students after graduation and staff. At the time of writing, more than half of all academic staff are on insecure contracts, reflecting a broader embrace of a neoliberal model both in higher education and in wider society where precarious work is becoming normalised (UCU, 2016).

Corporatisation has also impacted on the governance structures of universities. The traditional structure of university governing bodies such as Senates included a combination of academics and public representatives. Leadership posts, such as deans and vice chancellors, were filled by academics, who were therefore the people taking decisions about the way the organisation was run. Administrators were positioned as providers of support to academics. Strategic decisions were (ideally at least) informed by fundamental values held by universities such as collegiality and academic freedom, rather than being seen as value-neutral or economically efficient. Increasingly, such roles and decisions have been taken by people with full-time roles as managers, on a management career track (even if they come from an academic background) (Shepherd, 2018), with managerial decisions being guided by university strategies. As Shattock (2014) argues, over the past 50 years academics have lost substantial ground in relation to their autonomous roles in the governance of their own institutions, determination of their conditions of service, and regulation of standards and accountability.

Centralised assessment of the quality of research is another important factor influencing academics' writing and work lives. Since 1986, with the introduction of the Research Assessment Exercise (RAE), UK universities have had to compete for part of their research funding by engaging in regular exercises to assess and compare the quality of their research, and quality-related (QR) funding is allocated according to performance in these. Over the years, such research evaluation exercises (now called the Research Excellence Framework, REF) have become more significant and have distributed greater proportions of money (Stern, 2016).

The REF has such significance for a university's income and reputation that most institutions have policies aimed at ensuring their academics produce enough work of sufficient quality to score highly in it. For many universities, particularly research-intensive ones, the QR funding which the REF governs is an important part of their income stream. In addition, a high score on the REF links to rankings and league tables, which in turn affect an institution's ability to raise income from tuition fees.

The REF evaluates units (usually departments) in universities against the quality of three elements: their "outputs" – usually publications; the unit's "research environment", which takes into account a range of indicators including doctoral degrees awarded, research income gained, and research strategy and infrastructure; and case studies of evidence of the "impact" of the unit beyond academia. The "impact" criterion is relatively new, introduced in 2014, and was designed to introduce an element of public accountability to research making a difference in the world, the so-called "impact agenda". Responses to this expressed concern about unwarranted interference in the research agenda (Chubb, Watermeyer, & Wakeling, 2017). In the 2014 REF, the proportions the different elements contributed to the evaluation were 65% outputs, 20% impact, 15% environment, so publications form a particularly significant part of the assessment of the quality of research. Given the importance of high REF scores, most universities and departments have policies in place to encourage their academic staff to produce publications likely to perform well, particularly monographs with academic publishers and journal articles in high-impact peer-reviewed international journals. This results in pressure to meet these demands, and writing choices thereby become influenced by government policy and university strategy.

A final set of changes affecting higher education relates to the use and potential of digital technologies. These interact with the changes described above to reconfigure academic networks and collaborations (Castells, 2010) as well as the physical environment of the university. Academic offices become more like impersonal corporate spaces as university estates are refurbished and developed; dispersed international campuses are visited and communicated with in different ways from the local working environment (Temple, 2014). New digital tools facilitate distance and blended learning via VLEs and video conferencing (Goodfellow & Lea, 2013). As well as changing the nature of relationships with students and colleagues, digital technologies change the times and spaces within which academic writing is accomplished. Smartphones and other portable devices allow working on the move and continuity across different places and times. This book describes the impact of these changes on the working and writing lives of academics, and the implications of these transformations for knowledge production and for academic identities.

## Research on academic writing

Our project builds on a number of intersecting areas of research which can provide insights into academics' writing practices and how they are situated within broader cultural practices, intellectual traditions, and national policies. The most significant of these are described in this section. A wider literature which theorises the organisation of workplaces and of the professional writing work of "knowledge workers" of different kinds (e.g. Fenwick & Nerland, 2014; Taylor & Spicer, 2007; Van Marrewijk & Yanow, 2010) is useful for exploring the specifics of the higher education workplace context and the university academic's specialised role. Likewise, this study intersects with an extensive literature on the changes in digital technologies affecting university life at all levels (see Goodfellow & Lea, 2013).

The well-developed field of academic writing research (see Lillis & Scott, 2007) has mainly focused on students' learning – that is, the practices of apprentice writers in an assessment context. To date, only a few areas of research have paid attention to the writing of academics themselves. Notably, Swales (1998) carried out an unusual in-depth study of academic writing in three departments (IT support, botany, English language education) housed on different floors of the same university building. His "textography" describes the "routine writing business" on each floor of the building, combining close analysis of texts with interviews with scholars and analysis of their professional histories. The three departments represented three very different discourse communities, with differing orientations to time, vocabularies, text types, purposes, and rhythms of work. This study provides insight into academics' situated writing practices, but is specific to a particular setting and very much reflects the time at which it was written, given the subsequent rapid development of digital technologies. Swales revisited this work two decades later, writing an update on the three sites (McCarty & Swales, 2017; Swales, 2018, and see also the rereading by Gillen in the preface to the 20th anniversary edition). Swales' focus on the physical environment of academics writing is also worth revisiting in the light of the multiple, changing pressures on space to which university estates in the UK are responding. These include the need to accommodate increasing student numbers; to produce branded "signature" buildings that market the institution to students and funders; and to reconfigure learning and teaching spaces to allow access to digital resources (see Temple & Barnett, 2007).

Lea and Stierer (2009, 2011) carried out an interview-based study of lecturers' everyday writing as professional practice, working with 30 academics across three institutions. They looked at the range of writing demanded by the professional workplace, and the implications of these practices for academic identities and development. This work shares our perspective on universities as workplaces, on writing as practice, and on the value of a detailed approach focusing on naturally occurring texts and practices, although their research deliberately excluded scholarly writing. They found a very wide range of writing in academic workplaces, and demonstrate the role of writing in the construction of a pluralistic, situated, and fluid range of identities, challenging dominant conceptualisations of academic work.

Lillis and colleagues' long-term ethnographic work with academics in different European countries focuses particularly on multilingual scholars publishing in English (Lillis & Curry, 2010). This work describes the pressures on scholars around the world to publish in English. It explores the strategies they adopt to achieve this, and considers the implications of the global dominance of the English language in the production of knowledge.

Much work in academic writing analyses aspects of the language, genre, and structure used, in relation to discipline and discourse community (e.g. Hyland, 2012; Swales, 2004; Myers, 1990) and/or focuses predominantly on learning academic writing (e.g. Ivanič, 1998; Murray, 2015). The work examining disciplinary differences in the nature of the texts produced by academics focuses for instance on forms of argumentation or on the historical development of genres (Prior, 1998; Russell, 2002). Bazerman (2005) summarises the main contributions of this research: understanding the nature of scientific and technical writing; the socialisation of graduate students into the writing practices of their field; critiquing the rhetorical activities of particular fields and studying the history and sociology of sciences, particularly in the tradition of science and technology studies (see Latour, 1987).

Research into the impact of digital technologies on academics' writing is recent, but growing. For example, see Borgman (2007) and Goodfellow (2013) on digital scholarship; Corrall and Keates (2011) on the use of libraries and resource centres; and Fraiberg (2010) and Gourlay (2012) on changing knowledge practices in the digital university. Goodfellow and Lea's collection *Literacy in the Digital University* (2013) addresses many pertinent issues from a literacy studies perspective, including the changing nature of digital scholarship. We carried out an initial study about academics' writing six years before the study reported in this book, which provides a temporal perspective on the current research, having been carried out before the government-influenced impact agenda was imposed on English universities, and at a different stage of the shift to predominantly digital means of communication. The research is reported in part in the Goodfellow and Lea collection (see Satchwell, Barton, & Hamilton, 2013).

Martin Weller makes the point that all aspects of academic life are changing in developing the concept of the "Digital Scholar" (Weller, 2011). He uses the example of the role of digital media when writing an academic book, comparing what he did when writing a book in 2004 with his experience of producing the 2011 volume. He shows how every step of writing a book changed in that time. This is a finding that we would also apply to other aspects of academic life, including writing and submitting a paper; preparing, carrying out, and evaluating teaching; participating in a conference; impact work; and keeping student records. Digital tools and resources have reshaped the practices of every aspect of academic writing.

## Chapter by chapter outline

This first chapter has examined how universities are changing and the current pressures on those who work in the university sector, especially increasing managerialism in higher education along with new digital technologies. It has set out both the general approach taken and the background research framing this study, making the case for academic writing as centrally involved in processes of knowledge creation.

In the next chapter, Chapter 2, "Theories and methods for studying academics writing", we describe how we carried out the research. We outline the theoretical rationale for our design decisions and methodological approaches, before describing the specific data collection approaches we used: three distinct kinds of interviews with core participants; recording of writing processes using videography and observation; and broadening-out interviews with colleagues of our participants in the nine core sites. We explain the ways in which our own experiences as both researchers and academics were part of the data and how we exploited this through purposefully documenting them as auto-ethnography. We describe our approach to data analysis, using qualitative data analysis software and team coding, and explain how planned impact activities throughout the project informed its development. The aim of this chapter is both to explain our approach as clearly as we can, and to enable others who wish to carry out similar research to draw on our experiences.

Before focusing in on the key themes of the book, we move on in Chapter 3, "Days in the lives of academics, writing", to provide a taste of the realities of academics' professional lives and the importance of writing practices within these. We introduce some of our participants, focusing in on their writing lives at the day-to-day level, using vignettes to open up some of the key issues and questions which the rest of the book addresses. We show how "writing" has many different meanings to an academic and can be organised in different ways, in a range of locations, evoking an array of emotional responses from the writer.

The rest of the book addresses in turn key aspects of academics' lives which shape and are instantiated in their writing practices. We pursue themes introduced through these vignettes, including: the space and time of academic writing; disciplines, genres, and writing; changing tools and technologies; new social media; roles, relationships, and writing collaborations; and how people learn the diverse genres and practices of academic writing that this research has identified.

The vignettes of Chapter 3 show the significance of where people write, when people write, and how they arrange their lives to protect particular kinds of writing. In Chapter 4, "Academics writing in space and time", we move on to focus particularly on such questions of space, time, and boundaries. We show the relevance of the choices people make concerning the spaces they write in, and the influence of institutional decisions about space which are driven by different priorities. We have identified the usefulness for academics of being able to set boundaries to protect space and time for particular kinds of work, particularly knowledge-creation work of the kind that is, in fact, often highly valued by the institution. The data make a strong case for individuals having the autonomy to set boundaries in space and time to protect particular kinds of writing practices. This chapter also has implications for training and professional development, making explicit the value of thinking through the creation and management of boundaries to address the challenges of academic writing life.

These challenges play out in different ways in relation to different genres of writing and indeed in different disciplinary contexts, and Chapter 5, "Disciplines, genres, and writing", turns to consider more directly how discipline and genre frame academics' writing practices and how these are experienced by the academics in the study. It discusses how writing practices are distributed across areas of knowledge production, and how they are changing. We deal with discipline-based ideas about knowledge, and how it is created, and what forms of knowledge are valued, including the satisfactions and frustrations of concerns with impact. By exploring the differences between the experiences of our participants in maths, marketing, and history, we demonstrate how the knowledge traditions of the different disciplines value knowledge that is created and presented in different ways, challenging some of the underlying assumptions which can be made by institution-wide strategies and particularly by nationwide evaluation systems. The chapter also explores the diversity of writing all academics engage in, both within and beyond their disciplinary research writing, showing the multitude of genres which are part of academic professional life and the diversity and hybridity of these genres.

In Chapter 6, "Changing tools and technologies in academics' writing lives", we take a closer look at tools and technologies which are leading to changes in academics' writing and what it means to be an academic. This includes tools and platforms provided by universities such as VLEs and online library resources, as well as social media, smartphones, and portable devices which academics may bring into the work place from their everyday lives. Their deployment can lead to new practices and every aspect of academic work can be seen to be changing as a result of them. By exploring people's diverse stances towards tools and technologies, we show how a technology like email, which is often assumed to be a mundane communicative means, has turned out to loom large in academics' working lives, requiring a disproportionate commitment of time and energy to keep under control.

Chapter 7, "New social media genres: Marketing the academic self", continues the focus on contemporary communication changes associated with digital technology, moving on from tools and technologies to explore the new genres and practices associated with social media and their use in the academy. This chapter focuses on how social media have transformed the writing environment. It is now possible to make research writing public without going through the gatekeeper of a publisher, for instance on a blog; to communicate globally and publicly with a community of academic peers, for example using Twitter; and to publicise work that has been published in more traditional venues widely and rapidly. Public online identities are built up using personal webpages, academic networking sites, and participation in a range of social media spaces which can play a key role in building one's academic reputation. Such "digital scholarship" is associated with new genres of writing, on new platforms, for new audiences.

From this, it is clear that one of the key strengths of social media in the academic professional sphere is to facilitate collaboration with peers. Relationships and writing collaborations have always been important in scholarly work, but the tools, technologies, and media now available have opened up many new ways in which such relationships can be facilitated. In Chapter 8, "Relationships and collaboration in academic writing", we address the value of relationships and collaboration in academics' writing practices. While our study documented the experiences of individual academics, writing is not something which takes place in isolation. Much of the writing that academics do is done with, for, or even occasionally against, others. This chapter discusses the role that relationships play in academics' writing lives through their research, teaching, administration, and service roles and considers the range of people involved.

The previous chapters describe a picture of constant change in academics' writing practices through the ongoing introduction of new genres, demands, tools, and possibilities. In Chapter 9, "Learning academic writing: An ongoing process", we explore the ways in which academics learn in order to adapt to this rapidly changing context. We argue that the primary means is through informal, networked, collaborative learning, often connected with the important relationships, networks, and collaborations described in the previous chapter. The traditional model of training for an academic career – several years of focus on doctoral study, the production of a PhD thesis, and then perhaps a day or two of professional development events every year or so – does not provide the resources academics need to develop and understand the plethora of new writing practices they have to participate in as their careers develop. We identify the significance of departmental culture and context in the learning process, and we also identify certain aspects of writing, such as email management, for which the learning appears to be haphazard and individualised.

Chapter 10, "The futures of writing: Conclusions and implications", sums up and explores the implications of this research for individual academics, for people in positions of departmental management, for institutional management, and for higher education policy. We outline ways in which academic writing of all kinds can be supported, and ways of introducing a more positive writing culture in departments and institutions, including through writing groups, retreats, and communities. We explore the resonances of this research on higher education and academics in the UK for the wider international context. We reflect on how our understanding of contemporary academic writing practices can inform our understanding of the process of knowledge creation, and on how different conceptualisations of writing may be associated with different understandings of academic professional identity and the purposes of higher education.

# 2

# THEORIES AND METHODS FOR STUDYING ACADEMICS WRITING

## Framing the research: literacy studies and socio-material theory

As we explained in Chapter 1, this project approaches academic writing as a workplace practice. Following Lea and Stierer (2009, 2011) and Lillis and Curry (2010), we ask what do professional academics *do* in their academic writing work, and what does this writing mean to them? This sensibility guides our theoretical framing and the design of the study, to which we now turn. Our study is located at the intersection of literacy studies and socio-material theory. We outline these approaches and discuss how we have drawn from these complementary theoretical traditions in the conception, design, and implementation of our study and how they have guided the data analysis.

Researchers working in the fields of writing, literacy, and composition (such as McGrath & Kaufhold, 2016; Paltridge, Starfield, & Tardy, 2016; Tuck, 2018a) have investigated the multi-dimensional nature of the production of written language, and the broader social processes within which writing practices are embedded. Much of this work locates itself within the tradition of literacy studies, as formulated by Lea and Street (2006) who refer to the field as "academic literacies". Literacy studies views writing as emerging from a broad set of practices of literacy that are embedded in social contexts and historically located in time and space (Barton, 2007; Hamilton, 2012; Tusting, 2012). It is a "relational" theory of literacy that focuses on how people collaborate in acts of reading and writing, and the mediators and sponsors of written texts (see Brandt, 1998; Kalman, 1999). Within this research tradition, a distinction is made between "literacy events" and "literacy practices" (Barton & Hamilton, 2000, 2012). "Events" refer to observable and empirical moments in which some kind of engagement with texts (reading, writing, or talk around texts) is integral. In research, events can be a useful starting point, as interactions around a text can easily be documented. "Literacy practices" involve not just the writing activity and its resultant texts, but also the ideologies and patterns of behaviour surrounding the process, the attitudes and values that inform it, and the aspects of the broader social and historical context which has framed and shaped it (Tusting, Wilson, & Ivanič, 2000, p. 213). With its close observation of textually mediated interactions, literacy studies draws on and informs linguistic ethnography (Blommaert, 2013; Maybin & Tusting, 2011; Tusting, 2013).

Since its original formulation emerging from anthropology (Street, 1984), socio-cultural psychology (Scribner & Cole, 1981), and ethnographic socio-linguistics (Heath, 1983), literacy studies has undergone continuous development as it has responded to changes in the nature of literacy itself, especially in relation to digital technologies (see Snyder, 2002; Lankshear & Knobel, 2003; Baynham & Prinsloo, 2009). Responses include conceptual critiques (such as Brandt & Clinton, 2002) and application of the theory to new empirical contexts (e.g. Barton & Papen, 2010; Kalman & Street, 2013). Literacy studies accepts that academic writing practices take place within a changing communications landscape brought about by rapid digitisation and the globalisation of the higher education workplace (see Castells, 2010; Kress, 2013).

The theory has been extended to allow researchers to elaborate the ways literacy practices are connected across dispersed times and spaces to effect action. It now attends more seriously not only to the materiality of texts but to other kinds of non-human artefacts and resources that are part of the moment by moment unfolding of literacy events and activities. For example, Scollon's (2002) "mediated discourse" approach entails people drawing on a range of mediational means, engaging in a nexus of practice in which many different practices intersect. The practices through which writing tasks in academia are characterised and accomplished are therefore bound up with a multitude of "actors" that are not always situationally visible during writing activities. Actors can include such things as managerial directives, quality procedures, disciplinary conventions, departmental environment, and discipline-focused, thematic, or linguistic social communities. Professional writing practices may be acquired and sustained as much through engaging with "sponsors of literacy", as through formal training or education. Brandt develops this idea, defining sponsors of literacy as:

> any agents, local or distant, concrete or abstract, who enable, support, teach, model, as well as recruit, regulate, supress or withhold literacy – and gain advantage by it in some way.
>
> *(Brandt, 1998, p. 166)*

In a higher education context, literacy sponsors include colleagues and mentors who support academics' writing efforts, as well as publishers, reviewers, and editors who act as gatekeepers.

Practices set up multiple and sometimes contradictory expectations around writing which academics have to negotiate and make choices about in their day-to-day workplaces (Nygaard, 2017). This multiplicity presents researchers with the challenge of exploring the different sites through which these actors work and the different scales at which they interact and influence the minute by minute experience of academic life. To deal with these complexities, we use the complementary theoretical resources of literacy studies and socio-material theory to develop a new framework to inform contemporary literacy research.

Socio-material theory emerged from work in the field of Science, Technology and Society studies (STS) which explored the actual doing of science (e.g. Latour, 1987; Latour & Woolgar, 1986). This work showed the complexity of the processes of knowledge construction, and how much of the messy business and ephemeral work of a laboratory are excluded from the final stages of "fact production" and glossed over in scientists' final reports. Literacy studies and socio-material theory have much in common. Both approaches focus on vernacular, everyday activities, documented ethnographically, and offer methodological links with studies of everyday practice (e.g. Ingold, 2011; Shove, Pantzar, & Watson, 2012). Both focus on process and fluid constellations of actors rather than fixed structures. While literacy studies directs us to look at the ecology of practices in writing events (Barton, 2007), a socio-material understanding attunes us to look at how people and material artefacts are entangled, forming "assemblages" that give rise to certain kinds of writing, certain regimes of authority, and cultures of writing in a given department, institution, or disciplinary community. The idea of assemblage also denotes a concern with classifications, categories, and boundaries, seeing these as contingent, unstable, and permeable. In refocusing attention on the *changing configurations* of practices, socio-material theory takes us beyond the situated context of writing, and towards the network of actors (social, material, and political) implicated in the writing work and knowledge production of academics.

Attending to how this network of social, material, and political actors is drawn together in writing highlights the concrete specificities of the writing process. In the study reported here, people talk about the times and spaces in which they work, the resources, tools, and furniture they rely on to carry out their writing and how they move between these for convenience and comfort and to deal with the demands on their time. This brings into focus how writing routines are shaped and reveals how these are managed: the priorities, decision-making, challenges, setbacks, emotional labour, and collaborations that underpin the production of documents of different kinds. This is backstage work (see Star & Strauss, 1999) that is usually invisible to the final audience. This approach is especially revealing since higher education, as discussed above, is changing rapidly, and the aims, responses, and identities of those involved are various and also in flux.

Both literacy studies and socio-material theory engage with texts and their meaning-making capacities. Socio-material theory highlights the material aspects of texts, using the term inscription, which, as Latour explains, "refers to all the types of transformations through which an entity becomes materialized into a sign, an archive, a document, a piece of paper, a trace" (Latour, 1999, p. 306). Inscription solidifies meanings and circulates them, co-ordinating the work of diverse actors. Literacy theorists also understand this well and describe how social relations and purposes (ideas about the user and the usage) are encoded into texts (e.g. Ivanič, 1998). In this way, a textual artefact is "inscribed" with a certain pattern of action which later on will, to a greater or lesser extent, influence and determine the actual use of the artefact. Inscription thereby enables social action, helping to move forward intellectual and practical projects. Academics are entangled in this work of inscription both through the vocational interests and commitments they purposefully pursue in their professional communities, and by the institutional demands they are bound to satisfy as part of their employment. These motivations discipline their writing skills and shape their identities.

Socio-material theory has strongly influenced research on the human/ machine digital interface (e.g. Orlikowski, 2007; Suchman, 2007). This work has highlighted the more general point that both human and non-human actors are entangled in every social act. Rethinking social acts within a socio-material understanding de-centres the human as the sole agent of anything conceived as "social" (Bowker & Star, 2000; Callon, 2002; Fenwick, Nerland, & Jensen, 2012). Forms of writing are built upon and maintain their characteristics as the *effects* of such networked entanglements of actors and their practices. How knowledge is produced through writing within systems of higher education is therefore contingent upon such network effects that must be examined closely.

One important effect of these networks is how they sustain the regimes of authority in higher education which, over time, determine which forms of writing have importance and credence, and which do not. Writing from a socio-material perspective, Fenwick and Edwards (2014) argue that:

> Knowledge in higher education is codified and sedimented in a variety of repositories: as received concepts, textbooks, prescribed curricula, instruments such as a calibrated measuring tubes, technologies such as diagnostic machines or open access data bases, assessment forms, teaching protocols, even architecture.
>
> *(p. 36)*

It is through such socio-material assemblages that ways of "being an academic" and "doing writing" are realised and it is here that we need to look for traces of changing knowledge practices.

## Implications for research design and methodology

The approach described above has important implications for how we study literacy and writing empirically. In this section we summarise these implications as a bridge into the description of the work we carried out. The combination of literacy and studies and socio-material theory enables us to reformulate the set of propositions we used to guide our earlier work on literacy practices (see Barton & Hamilton, 2012, p. 7) as explained below.

1.  As Pardoe (2000) points out, a guiding methodological principle of both an ecological approach to literacy and an STS perspective is to adopt the principle of symmetry – attending in a non-evaluative, equitable way to all aspects of the phenomena we come across, regardless of how they are valued externally. This demands that we document and analyse details of *everyday experience*, including observable events which are mediated by written texts and from which broader social practices can be inferred. In the case of academics' writing work, this means our data includes not just prestigious forms of research writing, but also the mundane activities of producing quality assurance documents, student feedback, and administrative emails to colleagues.

2.  We need to continue to explore the detail of *how writing events are situated in time and space* drawing on studies of literacy (Lemke, 2000; Nespor, 2007; Swales, 1998; Prior & Shipka, 2003) and the broader insights of STS and social geographers about different temporalities and the physical features of environments for writing (Adam, 2008; Lefebvre, 1991; May & Thrift, 2003).

3.  In particular, we need to address how specific writing events are held together through *social relations* that coalesce in writing practices through networks of support, mediators, and sponsors (see Barton & Tusting, 2005). We need methods which can take account of the dynamic forces that mesh human and non-human actors together to accomplish writing. This includes resources and devices such as the informational infrastructure of digital technologies and libraries (Ivanič et al., 2009; Lea & Street, 1998).

4.  A further methodological demand is that we document how literacy practices are *purposeful and embedded in broader social goals and cultural practices*. Different literacies are associated with different domains and communities. The principal purposes of writing practices, and how a writer resolves tension between competing purposes and types of writing, can be interpreted in the light of a writer's broader professional commitments, and of the values they hold, for instance about the place of creativity and innovation in writing (Hamilton & Pitt, 2009).

5.  And research needs to address the patterning of writing practices by *social institutions and power relationships*, leading to some literacies

becoming more dominant, visible, and influential than others. These patterns can be traced from specific moments of writing outwards to identify the multiple human and non-human actors that animate them. For example, we can trace the links between completing a report on student evaluations of teaching with guidelines and procedures that originate from a distant body such as the Quality Assurance Agency and are enforced through local institutional rules and committees. Academic disciplines, departments, and institutions vary in the constraints and norms they impose on writers regarding how to carry out writing for research, teaching, administration, consultancy, and service purposes (Bazerman, 2005; Trowler, 2014). Thus, we need to look not just at the situatedness of academics' writing (i.e. what is happening in a very moment of writing), but also at the power relations and socio-cultural histories embedded within acts of writing. This includes the multiple and sometimes conflicting value-systems at the level of the departments in which academics work, their institutions and managerial imperatives, and more broadly their disciplinary communities.

6.   Finally, our approach to literacy practices demands that we take "the long view" of how these are *historically situated and changing*. Acts of writing are encapsulated moments in time which follow a chronology of events leading up to the present and into the future. Texts also have trajectories (Lillis & Maybin, 2017), they circulate and co-ordinate knowledge production across multiple actors (sites, people, tools, platforms, communities, etc.). This means they have historical roots, are established in long-term perspectives yet also pave the way for future writing. In this respect, Charles Bazerman argues that the establishment of the genre of the scientific article evolved from an established set of historical writing practices, which then evolved to shape – and continue to shape – the enterprise of science altogether, as discussed in Swales (1990). An investigation which tracks academics' writing practices must therefore take an historical approach and attempt to reveal the underlying physical and information architecture of contemporary literacy practices, and who and what is involved in them.

## From principles to design

These sensibilities and concepts led us to a set of questions that framed the design of our empirical study. In sum, we wanted to design a study that would reveal the material detail of changes in writing practices in the higher education workplace, viewing the university as a tangible, situated organisation which is networked regionally and globally. We set out to look at writing and the dynamics of knowledge creation in the changing academy, addressing the overarching question of how knowledge is produced and distributed through the range of writing practices academics engage in, including scholarly, pedagogic, administrative, and impact writing.

We looked for processes and explanations of how, where, when, with whom, and why academics write. Starting from the socio-material perspective on literacy studies outlined above, we explore how academics' writing practices are shaped by socio-material aspects of the situation, including the affordances of physical spaces and other material resources; social relationships with peers, colleagues, students, and managers; and how these practices are shaped by where they were located, both in terms of particular departments and universities, and also in terms of disciplinary locations. Because of the changing approaches to management associated with the corporatised university described in Chapter 1, attention to how managerial practices are shaping and co-ordinating academics' writing work is an important aspect of this. And, given the importance of transformations in communication made possible by digital technologies, it is essential to address the role of such technologies in shaping socio-material writing processes.

The ethnographic methods of literacy studies are necessary to uncover the everyday social practices of academics' writing and the infrastructures within which academics carry out their work. The traditional elements of literacy studies analysis described above – texts, events, and practices – are drawn on, enriched by some of the conceptual tools of socio-material theory, including notions of symmetry, assemblage, and inscription. This enables a finer examination of the entanglements of human and non-human actors that give different kinds of writing their specific characteristics and helps us link writing securely with wider knowledge creation practices.

Taken together, these approaches draw our attention to how texts circulate within and beyond the local university setting and between print, digital, and other modes of representation, and how participants perform everyday writing tasks and enact "being an academic" in organisational settings. This enables us to use the lens of writing practices to develop insights into the nature of academic and scholarly professional identities in the context of changing higher education in England.

## Methodological decisions and procedures

The writing practices of academic staff in nine sites were followed for over a year, through a combination of interviews, close ethnographic observation of both online and offline writing activities, and analysis of the wider organisational context within which the writing took place.

Phase one of the project entailed a series of three distinct interviews carried out with 16 core academics working at the three different English universities targeted for the study. These academics provided the point of entry for the study. In order to examine how the participants' writing and context varied by institution, we worked in three different universities: a large nineteenth-century city-based, research-intensive university, a smaller campus based, research-intensive university dating from the 1960s and a large teaching-intensive urban university.

Within these universities, we worked with academics in three disciplines: mathematics, history, and marketing. The disciplines were chosen so as to have what can broadly be described as a STEM (science, technology, engineering, and mathematics) discipline, a humanities discipline, and a professional/applied discipline (Becher & Trowler, 2001). We also carried out piloting work in social science departments.

In choosing the disciplines, we were conscious of the fact that there are many ways to divide up disciplines. Research on higher education expresses reservations about the extent to which disciplines can be essentialised (Becher & Trowler, 2001; Trowler, Saunders, & Bamber, 2012). Trowler (2014) notes that while disciplinary categories are a useful research heuristic, the everyday work of academics is affected as much by national and global factors as by disciplinary culture, and that such cultures are highly contingent on context. Different subject areas within disciplinary groupings have much in common, but also many unique and contrasting features. One could argue, for example, that mathematics is a marginal "science" discipline, since, unlike some other STEM subjects, pure mathematics at least is less concerned with direct empirical experimentation. Likewise, Kuteeva and McGrath (2015) have found that the rhetorical patterns in pure maths research articles differ from those in many others in hard science disciplines, as described by Hyland (2005). However, in the same way every discipline has its own characteristic features which make it distinctive within its broader grouping. We initially set out to use the academic department as a working unit, but we found there was a complex relationship between departments and disciplines. Some of our participants had received their PhDs in one discipline, but were working in a department labelled as a different one. The organisation of the different universities split disciplines up differently, with broadly based schools being a more salient institutional division in the teaching-intensive university than smaller departmental-scale units. In terms of this project, though, such blurred distinctions did not cause an insuperable problem. Our goal was not to recruit participants as representative of disciplines, but to ensure we were working with academics from a wide range of disciplinary contexts. The spread of academics over the three universities and, broadly speaking, three disciplines gave nine research sites.

Participants were recruited from these research sites by contacting them directly, in some cases through the research team's professional networks, and in other cases by contacting them directly via their institutional webpages and inviting them to participate. In this sense, the sample is necessarily somewhat self-selecting. Nevertheless, we tried to achieve a reasonable spread of participants in terms of gender, nationality, and professional roles. We use the three levels of academic posts of lecturer, senior lecturer, and professor commonly used in England including at our three research sites. Participants ranged in experience from early career staff through to senior professors. The initial sample of 16 core participants consisted of seven professors, three senior lecturers, and six lecturers. Four out of the 16 core participants were women; this reflected to a degree the gender balance of the departments studied, all of which had a majority of men. (In recruiting participants to phase three, we made specific efforts to redress imbalances in gender, language use, and contractual status in our broader sample.)

## Phase one: differently focused interviews

Phase one of the study documented the diversity of writing practices carried out by our core participants, including writing for research, for teaching, for administration, and for impact. It consisted of three semi-structured interviews with the core participants, each lasting between 60 and 90 minutes. These drew on a range of methods including techno-biographical interviews, tracking of specific events, and discussions around pieces of writing. During this time, we also carried out auto-ethnographic investigations of the research team's own practices (see Chang, 2008).

### Walk-along interviews

The first interview was an adaptation of a "go-along" interview (Garcia, Eisenberg, Frerich, Lechner, & Lust, 2012) which we called a "walk around". This is an interview technique which incorporates a walking tour of the participant's workplace as part of the discussion. This kind of data collection therefore helped us to understand the influences of the material space, institutional resources, and working environment on their knowledge creation practices. While interviewing participants we observed office spaces, some of which were shared, we passed printer rooms, social spaces, and walked through corridors with notices on the walls and doors. Each of these places which constitute the working environment are aspects of the culture of writing and knowledge production in the working lives of the participants. This part of the first phase of data collection was accompanied by photographs, written fieldnote observations, and collections of any relevant documentation related to writing, such as policies on digitisation and research impact.

### Techno-biographical interviews

The second, "techno-biographical", interview focused on the participants' use of digital technologies at different points in their life history and in different domains of their lives. A techno-biography is one way to research a participant's lived experience with digital media, phases of change over time, and how and why particular habits of use emerge. Works in early cybercultural studies (Henwood, Kennedy, & Miller, 2001) draw attention to techno-biographies as "accounts of everyday relationships with technology" (p. 11). In a detailed argument for their deployment in qualitative research, Kennedy

(2003) presents techno-biographies as a means to solicit "what it feels like to live certain experiences of digital multimedia from the inside" (p. 121), and to uncover how "privileged and non-privileged identity positions" emerge in and through practices with digital media (p. 121).

More recent work in the field of literacy studies and social media practices presents a variant of this method which focuses the interview towards literacy practices. For example, Page, Barton, Unger, and Zappavigna (2014) describe what they call a "techno-linguistic biography" as "a participant-centred way of documenting change over time in social practices, especially as these relate to people's lived experiences with technology and their language use online" (p. 128). In this respect, techno-biographical interviews should be reflexive in nature (Barton & Lee, 2013), and support broader ethnographic studies in a social practice approach to literacy and writing (Barton, Hamilton, & Ivanič, 2000). Techno-biographies gave us a vital window into academics' lived experiences with technology, the subtle and nuanced ways in which the use of different digital technologies enables and constrains practices of knowledge creation.

The focus of our techno-biographical interviews was on our academic participants' use of digital technologies and the affordances and constraints this brought to their working lives. Building on Barton and Lee (2013, p. 72), our interviews began with the following key areas and questions:

1.  Identification and discussion of how they wrote their first ever piece of scholarly work, alongside writing activities related to teaching and recordkeeping at the start of their academic career.
2.  How collaborative writing occurs, and how this has changed over the years.
3.  Managing delineations between professional and personal online profiles and activities, and hours of work.
4.  How they respond to institutional directives regarding digital and social media.

This led to discussion of how the tools and resources they made use of had changed over time, and if and how this had affected their writing practices today. Participants explained how they felt about their use of technologies and their different stances on its use in different aspects of their professional life (see Chapter 6 on changing tools and technologies). Interesting stories also emerged of why and how our participants began using various social media, and how they managed some of the contradictions inherent in their use of digital technology (see Chapter 7 on social media).

## Day-in-the-life interviews

Finally, the third interview focused on a specific day in the life of the participants to discuss the practices and networks they engage with. This involved the participants elucidating their writing activities within a recent day or couple of days with the researcher (see Chapter 3) and allowed to us to examine in detail the times and locations of all (work- and non-work-related) writing practices in a "typical" work day. We also heard from the participants how routines and networks are established in their regular patterns of work and the everyday challenges which they face.

## Phase two: videography

When it comes to capturing how writing occurs in practice, traditional ethnographic methods of observation used alone can fall short because some practices are hidden or inaccessible. For example, in describing an act of writing, participants are unlikely to mention aspects such as the use of multiple texts, tabs, search engines, and other resources simultaneously. In the second phase of the research, we therefore attempted to capture academics' writing activities unfolding in real time, along with the surrounding interactions by using a video-based method with its roots within the fields of ethnomethodology and workplace studies (e.g. Luff, Hindmarsh, & Heath, 2000; Bhatt, 2017b). This enabled us to capture the moment-by-moment practices that were drawn on in daily acts of writing work and to identify which actors were mobilised, and how, for writing to happen.

We asked eight of our core participants to allow us to record an act of writing. Participants worked on texts of their own choosing, using tools in line with their usual practices. Before the writing session, we installed the screen-recording software Camtasia and a webcam on our participants' computers. This captured a screen-in-screen audio and video recording of all interactions during the writing event, such as typing, deleting, copy-pasting, browsing, as well as vocalisations, discussions, gestures, interruptions, and how time was managed within the writing event.

This phase of the project involved particular ethical and practical challenges. First, it was not always easy to get permission to install software on institutional machines. Second, not everyone felt comfortable with the idea of their every move being recorded. In one case, we resolved these issues by using a different approach, observing the participant's writing: simply sitting in the room with them and taking detailed notes rather than recording their on-screen activity. Another issue related to ethics. We had sought the informed consent of our immediate participants, but this did not take into account other people brought into the particular writing acts being recorded. Information about co-writers, emails that interrupted writing work, the use of web searches when writing, and so on were vital for us to understand the multiple practices converging in moments of writing, yet these practices involved others who had not consented to participate, and often meant using confidential passwords to log into different sites. We addressed this by giving participants the option to pause and restart their recording using a pause/

restart icon in the taskbar menu. Participants were able to inform us if there were any sections of the recording that they wanted us to delete (e.g. password entries and sensitive emails). We also used editing features to blur sections of the screen recording when making them public, for instance in presentations, and to anonymise participants, as in Figure 2.1.

To prepare the video data for analysis, Camtasia screen capture files were converted to mpeg format. We then produced detailed summary logs of the activities and interactions during the writing session. This enabled us to identify the patterns in the video data and the key moments that we wished to focus on, with time references in the logs enabling easy reference back to the original video data, as in Table 2.1.

## Phase three: broadening out

The third and final phase of data collection entailed broadening our sphere of interest out from the core 16 participants to interview other academics, heads of department, managers, and administrative staff. We tried, where possible, to include the head of department and a member of administrative staff, as well as up to three academic colleagues. In some cases, sites were organised into schools rather than departments, and the head of school was unable to participate; where we could, we recruited other members of staff with management responsibilities. The roles of administrative staff also varied from one institution to another. Some administrative staff served several departments, and were located in centralised hubs in different buildings from the academic staff they worked with. It was also difficult to recruit administrative staff to participate in

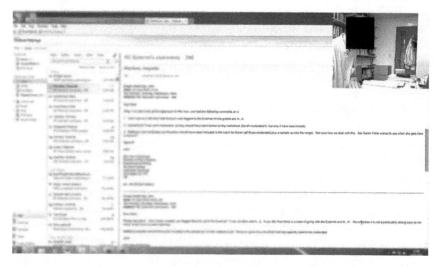

FIGURE 2.1 Example of screen-in-screen recording

**TABLE 2.1** Extract from videolog

| Participant: | James Gibson |
| --- | --- |
| Filename: | UniB_MRKT_2016-02-15_JGibson_Videolog |
| Date, place and time: | 15 February 2016; His office at Uni_B; late afternoon (beginning c. 3:30 pm) |
| Working on: | A paper with a co-author |
| Illustrates: | How his edits are both changes to the text and part of a conversation with the author; how he gives instructions to the co-author; how he moves from atomistic linguistic edits at the start to more rhetorical moves near the end; a 35–40 minute interruption to deal with an online student. |
| Typical for participant? | In terms of location and time – yes |

| | Time | Moment |
| --- | --- | --- |
| Summary of video, identifying and locating key moments | 0.00– 1.00 | JG opens the word document "[title]" Scrolls to 4th line of text (the abstract) and corrects a punctuation typo by deleting an extra period after a sentence (00:53) Highlights the entire abstract to ascertain the number of words (00:56) |
| | 1.00– 2.00 | Scrolls to next page (1st page of the article itself) Takes hand off mouse and crosses arms Pauses and clicks on parenthetical reference ([ref]) in 2nd paragraph (01:24) Scrolls to page 2 without making any changes (01:36) Scrolls slowly down page 2 |
| | 2.00– 3.00 | Scrolls onto page 3 (02:11) Pauses at beginning of 2nd paragraph of page 3 and reads aloud (02:20) Scrolls one or two lines down to make next section (Conceptual Framework) visible (02:40) Scrolls back to top of paragraph 2 (02:47) Clicks at beginning of paragraph (02:49) Highlights first 2 sentences of paragraph 2 (from "the main findings of this study" … to … "and which are less influential") (02:50) Adds comment using Word Review function. First comment using Word's Comment function is addressed to self/co-authors. It is about an early section where the main findings are previewed, and relates to need to reflect changes made to the overall argument and the addition of new data. Types comment: "Need refinem...." (02:56) Corrects spelling in comment. Deletes "em" and retypes "... refining in light of the reshuffling of ..." (02:59) |

our interviews, given the limits they faced on their time and autonomy. In the large research-intensive university in particular, as a result of these constraints, it did not prove possible to recruit appropriate administrative staff for phase three of the project. It was also not straightforward to recruit academic staff from within the same discipline in all cases. For example, some institutions had departments centrally linked to our target disciplines, with roles such as "lecturer in mathematics", while others had only a handful of staff teaching specialisms within broader, more interdisciplinary subject areas. Despite this complexity, we recruited between one and seven additional staff members at each research site, giving us a total of 39 participants for phase three, in addition to the 16 core participants recruited in phase one.

## Data analysis

Interviews from phases one and three were transcribed and anonymised before being entered into the qualitative research software ATLAS.ti (version 7.5.10) for analysis, as were observational notes, photographs, and summary logs of the phase two videography data. Documents were grouped into "families" by participant, by institution, and by discipline, to allow us to easily work with sub-sets of the data.

The data were coded by the research team, with the coding of documents being allocated and discussed at the regular project team meetings. All five members of the research team had access to all the data on ATLAS.ti; the Box cloud storage system of the university was used to store and share the ATLAS.ti hermeneutic units, which were updated with new documents and merged coding each month. Regular discussions of coding and analysis in team meetings provided ongoing testing of the validity of the findings which were emerging. (See Figure 2.2 for an example of a photograph from the data with coding alongside.)

The initial coding scheme we used was based on the primary objectives of the project, and was applied and refined through discussion as more data were analysed and new themes emerged. Phases one and two involved the development of a coding structure responsive to the data, starting with a small number of main codes and adding and refining more descriptive codes in response to the data. By the time we reached phase three of the project, the coding framework was well established and reflected and supported our developing theoretical understandings. While a few additional codes emerged from phase three, for the most part the coding in phase three used the framework which had emerged from the earlier phases, to fulfil the purpose of testing out the understandings developed on the basis of work with our core participants with a larger group of people, and to extend out from individuals to address disciplines and institutional contexts as units of analysis where appropriate. The phase three interview data were, therefore, read through again as the project evolved, summarised, and incorporated into the arguments to emerge from our analysis of phases one and two. In this way, we

**FIGURE 2.2** Example of a coded photograph

were able to verify preliminary findings as well as compare and contrast data across the different research sites and contexts.

The final coding structure consisted of 515 codes, most of which were grouped. These groups identified data relating to: boundaries; cultures; digital devices; digital platforms; disciplines; divisions of labour; evaluations; genres; modes; persons; places; practices; resources; spaces; strategies; tools; and work types. There were also some stand-alone codes, for instance: resistance; REF; management and autonomy; and learning.

We used the coding to identify the themes which emerged as most salient in the data, to identify places where counterpoints to these themes were located, and to enable us to generate smaller and more focused sets of extracts from the data which related directly to specific issues. We read these multiple times, manually annotated and discussed them. The most salient themes form the basis of the chapters which follow: space, time, and boundaries (drawing particularly on the coding for boundaries, places, spaces, resources, work types); disciplines and changing genres (drawing on disciplines, genres); tools, technologies, and platforms (drawing on digital devices, digital platforms, tools, modes); social media (drawing on digital platforms); relationships and collaboration (drawing on division of labour and persons); and learning. Some of the codes (cultures; evaluations; management; practices; strategies) were relevant across many themes. In some cases, the language of the data became the focus of analysis, for instance in the identification of patterns of metaphor use around email or stances adopted towards different technologies. These are discussed in the chapters that follow. Where quotations from the data have been used in the text, we chose quotations from these data groupings which we judged to effectively illustrate the points being made.

## Auto-ethnography

We are, of course, academics ourselves, participating in and experiencing the very changes we are researching, and writing about them. It was therefore important that as well as our work with all the participants we should question and understand our own roles, our own positions as researchers and as academics. This auto-ethnographic perspective brings the self into the research methodology, as we analysed our own practices, experiences, and techno-biographies, not just those of the people being researched. We used the same methods to research our own practices as we used with the research participants, with each member of the research team, including the project administrator, both interviewing and being interviewed by another member. We kept fieldnotes on our own practices at various points through the study. As we developed our understandings of the patterns and themes emerging from the data, we set our own experiences in the light of these understandings and reflected explicitly on these in team meetings and in our own fieldnotes. These discussions continued throughout the process of writing this book and we would argue that they prompted us to generate new and deeper analyses.

## Impact activities in the research sites

The project also included a series of events within the universities we worked with, to feed back emerging findings as the project was being carried out. These events brought together staff of varying levels of seniority and research students to open up focused discussions on academic professional development and working culture within the contemporary university. Importantly, the events also provided us with an opportunity to discuss the relevance and validity of our findings with participants. We organised a two-day residential writing retreat for staff at our participating institutions, during which we provided brief input on different aspects of the project's findings, as well as having more traditional structured sessions in which academics could set and share their writing goals, and enjoy protected time to work on a piece of writing.

In the chapters that follow, we present our findings according to the main themes mentioned above. In order to provide a more holistic sense of the realities of academics' writing practices we begin in the next chapter by introducing our core participants, describing some "days in their lives".

# 3

# DAYS IN THE LIVES OF ACADEMICS, WRITING

In the chapters that follow, we identify and discuss various themes which have arisen from our study of academics' writing practices. In order to interpret these themes in context, we start by introducing you to some of our participants and take you through their everyday writing practices. In our third interview in phase 1 of the research, we asked our core participants to log the writing they engaged in in one recent day, and then to talk us through that writing. Most of the vignettes below are drawn from this interview. We chose for inclusion in the chapter the vignettes that best illustrate the diversity of a "day in the writing life" of an academic, show the pressures that people are facing and how they respond to them, and introduce some of the themes which we will be exploring in further detail as the book proceeds. (All references to participants' names throughout the book are pseudonyms.)

---

### Clearing away the small tasks

Ian Fairclough lectures in mathematics at a research-intensive university. On the July morning in focus, he got up and checked his emails at 8.30 am, using a relatively new BlackBerry phone which he found much quicker for such checks than having to switch on his laptop. He likes to start the day "tidying up" his emails, getting on with any little things which need to be dealt with – on this day, writing a reference for a student for a Master's application – and "cleaning away" anything that has been dealt with.

At this time of the year, his working rhythm was very different from the middle of a teaching term. Summer was the time of year he focused on research writing. He would often try to work from home, but on this day he had a commitment to attend a colleague's talk at the university and a PhD supervision. After writing the student reference, he spent some time working at home on one of his main writing tasks for the day, a funding application for a conference, on his laptop, and then came in to attend the talk at 11 am before going back to his office.

For the second time that day, he began by clearing out emails, and then went back to his laptop to continue work on the funding application. This was a collaborative project with two other mathematicians, and he was late doing his part after being ill the previous week, so it had become a priority. He was working on the part where he needed to refer to previous research to justify the need for the conference, and had nine tabs open on the laptop linking to recent relevant research papers – hence the need to bring the laptop into the office. He was working on the case for support using LaTeX and would shortly be uploading his source code to Google Drive for the other mathematicians he was working with, before clearing it with the university research support office and uploading the finalised application to the Research Councils' Je-S submission system. This was challenging work, requiring thought and reading, but was not original mathematics. He also spent some of the day working on minor textual checks and corrections for a jointly authored article which was nearly complete. This was less challenging work which he could do by scribbling on a hard-copy printout, while on the bus for instance, enabling him to fit it in.

After the PhD supervision in the afternoon, he had to return home at around 5.30 because he had forgotten his laptop charger, but planned to continue working at home after that.

Ian's day shares many of the common patterns we identified amongst our participants. Beginning the day checking a smartphone, usually for emails, was normal for most people we spoke to, many of them starting to do this much earlier than 8.30 am – apart from the few who had made a deliberate decision not to. Emails are described as something that needs constant "tidying up" or "clearing out"; housework-related metaphors to which we will return in Chapter 6.

Ian uses technology to work fairly seamlessly across home and work locations, although this can be scuppered by practicalities such as the absence of the appropriate charger. Technology – Google Drive and Je-S, the UK Research Councils' online research proposal submission system – also enables him to work collaboratively with people across different institutions, with shared and expected use of LaTeX enabling distant sharing of mathematical symbols as well as alphabetical text. Nevertheless, pen and paper still have a place in his working life, with the affordances of hard copy opening up his daily commute as another potential space for writing.

Ian's work has distinct temporal rhythms, both in the day and in the year. He plans to get easy tasks done early on in the day and continues with more challenging work later, and this was his usual pattern. There are also clear patterns in his year: for example, he uses summer as his normal time for research writing. In addition to his own rhythms, though, his work is shaped by deadlines and plans shared with other people, and co-ordinating these can be challenging when faced with personal contingencies such as illness.

Ian's rhythms and practices seem to fit closely with what we might expect from an academic's writing life. As we shall see from some of the other examples, however, academics' writing lives vary a great deal and people face a wide range of different challenges.

## Meetings and multitasking

Gareth Waring is a more senior mathematician, also at a research-intensive institution, where he occupies a spacious office. At a similar point of the year, his daily experiences were very different. He played a key role in a doctoral training centre, and July was no quieter on the teaching front than any other time of year – in fact, it was possibly more intense, since there were more training days over the summer because of the availability of rooms at the university. For Gareth, October tended to be a quieter time when he could focus more on research reading and writing, once the new PhD students had been settled in and before reviews were due for the longer-established ones.

He started the day by following up from a meeting with a member of the university Senior Management Team at 5 pm the day before, which focused on the space needs of his centre. His first writing task for the day was therefore to send various emails and reports to the university Estates management. This delayed his first appointment, an annual appraisal meeting with a junior member of staff. The appraisal meeting required reports to be completed afterwards, which he fitted in around his other meetings as the day progressed.

Most of the rest of the day was spent in meetings with PhD students. In the first meeting, Gareth was going through edits on a joint paper written with one of his students, agreeing a response to referees' comments (much of his published writing around this time was jointly written with PhD students). This was a detailed and systematic process, writing together on his student's laptop, agreeing on changes a sentence at a time before the student worked on the sentence onscreen. During these gaps, Gareth would "get on with email for a couple of minutes" before returning to the student's laptop to check the changes.

The other two supervision meetings were less intensive in writing terms. Instead, Gareth found himself using pen and paper to scribble images and diagrams to support the discussions he had with students. After these meetings, he finished writing the report from the appraisal, and wrote some reviews on PhD students in the centre who he had recently met with to discuss their progress.

In the evening, he continued to work on his email, emailing Estates at 11 pm to make some requests about furniture for the new spaces. This was a typical pattern for him: with his days often filled up with meetings, emailing in the evening was necessary to keep on top of his inbox. He often found himself clearing the least important emails first, to get them out of the way, and tried to practise responding to everything within two days. The problem with this strategy was that some of the more important and difficult emails sometimes sat in his inbox for longer and could get overlooked.

We see some similarities between Gareth and Ian's experiences, but also some important differences. The annual rhythms of the year are very different. Both are shaped by teaching commitments, but where Ian's writing year is framed by the undergraduate calendar, Gareth's is the reverse of this. Both show the same orientation to keeping on top of email, talking about it using similar "clearing" metaphors, using small gaps of time between other tasks and at the ends of the day to do this (see Chapter 6 for further discussion of email metaphors). However, where Ian starts his day by clearing out emails, Gareth does this in the evening, opening up the possibility for email conversations to extend long into the night.

Like Ian, much of Gareth's research writing is collaborative, but where Ian worked with mathematicians in other institutions, Gareth worked predominantly with his own PhD students, supporting their career development and publishing mathematics from their PhD projects. Discussions are supported by pen and paper scribbles, rather than by using technologies for distant communication, although technology is still central to the production of the actual draft paper. Using technology collaboratively for writing is, for Gareth on this day, a close face-to-face encounter of writing together on a laptop, rather than sharing at a distance.

Because of his senior responsibilities, much of Gareth's writing during the day was made up of correspondence with management and facilities, and he uses the institutional genre of "report" to record decisions and to try to ensure that these are followed up in reality. Much of this work is framed by the many meetings that he attends, which require written preparation and follow-up in a timely way, shortly before and shortly after the meetings. The temporal positioning of the meetings therefore structures and limits his choice about which writing tasks can be done when, and which he can prioritise.

## Working from home

Rebecca is a historian at a research-intensive institution. Her "ideal" day would be a day on sabbatical, or during vacation when marking is finished, which she would spend writing and researching in an upstairs room at home in her pyjamas, interrupted only by going downstairs for a regular cup of tea. However, these days were rare. Typical days were more "hectic", beginning with checking emails at 6 am on her phone as soon as her alarm went off.

Generally, Rebecca preferred to work at home as much as possible, where she would not be subject to interruptions. However, she had been encountering problems with her laptop recently which meant that she was having to work far more in the office than she felt comfortable doing. On the day she was interviewed, in early September, she was in her office, focusing on teaching preparation, in order to be able to take a holiday at the end of the vacation period (before term started in early October). Her teaching-related writing for the day included emails about preparing courses and sorting out finances from a summer academy she had organised; updating her sites on the virtual learning environment (VLE) by going through her digital folders of teaching materials, uploading the ones she wanted, and deleting those she didn't; writing multiple course descriptions, for the VLE, for the undergraduate handbook, and for the course packs for each course, saying, "annoyingly the university, and then the faculty, and then the department, want us to produce the same piece of information in a number of different ways". She also did some research-related writing: working on an application form for a travel scholarship to support writing her next book and completing the transcription of historical manuscripts. She returned home around 5 pm, but continued with her writing there, as she would "invariably" do.

While Rebecca's example writing day took place during the university vacation, it is clear to see how much this is shaped by the needs of the upcoming undergraduate term, and how far it is from her "ideal" research writing day. Rebecca felt very strongly that working from home was preferable to working in her office (discussed further in Chapter 4), but, as with Ian's problems with his charger, her choice of working location was constrained by difficulties with the material technology.

The number of different types of writing that she engages in in the course of a single day is quite striking: financial correspondence; teaching materials; application form; transcription; research writing; and course descriptions, several for the same course written in slightly different ways, which multiplies her workload. (The wide range of genres of writing our participants engaged in, and the multiple sources they come from, will be discussed further in Chapter 5.) Unlike Ian and Gareth's collaborative research writing described above, all of the writing Rebecca describes is done by herself alone, although much of it is in response to or in preparation for work with other people (students or administrators). Much of her teaching-related writing is destined for the VLE, making teaching materials a public document open to those on the course at any time, rather than an ephemeral support for a teaching and learning interaction.

She works long hours to keep on top of these multiple demands. Like Ian, she begins early in the day by checking her emails on her phone, describing this as symptomatic of the "hectic" nature of her working days. And, like both Ian and Gareth, her writing day extends after she returns home into the evening.

---

### Daily routines

Collin Whitworth is a historian at a research-intensive university. Like many of our participants, he starts every day (including weekends) by checking his email, describing himself as an "email junkie". He would receive on average around 20 work-related emails a day which would require some thought and action. He tended to deal with the most recent emails first, and ones which had come in earlier could sit there for a while before they were addressed.

On the day of the interview, before he came in to work, he wrote some comments on a colleague's early stage research grant application, as part of his role in the department which requires him to support people in their research. He was keen to encourage the colleague to apply for European funding and so they had been identifying "big ideas" which had emerged from a recent period of research leave.

He then came into the university and taught a class. This required some additional organisational writing beforehand, creating an attendance sheet and grouping students using a table beforehand, changing the names on the one he had used in the previous year and uploading it to the VLE, and taking notes on their group discussions during the class to feed into plenary discussion at the end. The PowerPoint slides he used for the teaching had been edited the week before from last year's version, and were then uploaded after the class.

Teaching was followed by an office hour, when he spent half an hour talking with a student and then some time arranging books in his room, which he had recently moved into. He was sharing a room temporarily with another colleague while the building was being refurbished. The rest of the afternoon was spent completing a document for another university assessing their performance in the previous REF and making recommendations towards the next one, and finally working on a blog post. After getting home at around 5.30, he spent some more time checking emails and doing some administrative work in the evening.

---

Collin's day illustrates some working patterns common to many of our research participants. He makes no clear distinction between work time and non-work time. Work happens from the moment he gets up, when he checks his email, and continues into the evening. He works both at home and at the university, doing similar kinds of tasks in both places. Despite his relatively low email load compared to some of our other participants, he is very aware of the pull of email and uses the metaphor of addiction to describe his relationship with it. Some of his workday is spent coping with changes relating to a refurbishment and office move. His day mixes a wide range of types of writing, and in these we see emerging some of the themes we will discuss in more depth later in the book.

The influence of the REF on his everyday writing is evident both in the strategies he is considering as he comments on his colleague's research grant (looking for "big ideas") and, more directly, in the additional work he has taken on as a REF reviewer for another university, which gives him status and additional income as well as an insight into another university's approach, but also adds to his workload.

In his teaching-related writing we see the importance of the technologies of contemporary university teaching – in this case, the VLE and the PowerPoint. Both enable him to draw on his resources from previous years, in making administrative tasks quicker (updating the table of names) and in enabling content to be updated easily. At the same time, the blended nature of his teaching, with both content and organisational materials needing to be uploaded to the VLE, adds an additional layer of writing tasks which need to be synchronised with the face-to-face teaching encounter (see Chapter 6 for further discussion of such tools and technologies).

The blog post he writes at the end of the day represents a relatively new genre for him. Where his research writing had for years mainly consisted of chapters and journal articles, he had recently been receiving requests from media organisations for shorter pieces as his historical work touched on a contemporary current affairs issue; hence the blog post, and he had also recently joined Twitter. He found this new online writing and public profile both satisfying and anxiety-provoking. We will address the new online genres academics are engaging with in more depth in Chapter 7.

### Finding the printer, finding the papers

Brian Dow lectures in maths at a teaching-intensive university where he shares an office with one other colleague. On the day in focus he started teaching at 10 am, with an hour-long lecture followed by tutorials lasting two hours, one of which he taught. Aiming to come in at 9.30 am to miss the traffic, he had time at home to finish preparing the handouts for the tutorials, on a desktop computer. He also sent an email to a moderator relating to an upcoming exam board for a different module.

His major challenge for the morning was to figure out where he was going to print out the handouts. The printer near his office was not reliable, and using that one would require him to go up and down a set of stairs to check whether the documents were printing properly. He did not have time for this, so instead sent the handouts for printing at the end of the lecture to a printer located in the building where the tutorials were held, a fair distance from his office. If this worked, he could give them out to the tutors at the start of the tutorials; but he had to trust his local knowledge that this distant printer would prove more reliable than his local one.

After the tutorials, he registered students' attendance. One student had a query about a missing exam paper, having sat the exam under alternative arrangements, so he then had to go on a hunt for the paper, starting in the administration hub for the student's department. Eventually, the papers turned up in his pigeonhole, which was full of junk mail and rarely used; he was surprised he had not received an email to indicate that it was there.

He marked some hard copies while eating lunch out of the office. He deliberately spreads out marking, doing a little bit every now and again, aiming to get the marking done well before the exam board in case of any issues with the marks. He does worry about carrying hard copies of tests and exams around with him, but finds it very boring to sit marking at a desk. Then he returned to his office and sent some emails, telling the student their exam paper had been found and responding to some student enquiries.

He described this as a fairly typical day in the teaching term. In the summer, he might get a chance to work on research, but would also be spending time updating teaching notes and preparing assessments. It was always a challenge for him to get back into the momentum of doing research. Much of his research involved software development, and he needed to have a few hours without any other high-pressure work to make progress on that.

We can see in Brian's account a clear difference between the typical day at the teaching-intensive institution and those described so far at the research-intensive institution. Almost all of Brian's writing tasks on the day in focus are related to teaching, teaching administration, and assessment. He is very directly involved in assessment, personally going to hunt down a missing exam paper and being very aware of exam boards. His emails all relate to either contact with students or to assessment. The major challenge for him on this day comes in the immediate practical logistics of producing the teaching materials in physical form; the temporal flexibility afforded him to come in later to miss the traffic combined with the limitations of his local printer mean that he has to make some quick and slightly risky decisions about printing close to the lecture space.

## Managing email pressures

Diane Simmons is a senior academic in marketing at a research-intensive university. She is committed to many writing projects, both internal to her university and externally: writing collaborative journal articles, producing commissioned reports, doing external research projects and consultancies, and reviewing journal articles. She also has significant administrative responsibilities within her department. All of these involve working with other people, and the majority of the related communications occur by email. As a result, the volume of emails she deals with is huge. It is not unusual for 200 emails to come in each day that she needs to deal with. On the day we interviewed her, she had 436 unread emails in her inbox. She has a range of ways to manage this: sending very quick responses – "no chit-chat"; setting times for dealing with email, and times when she won't deal with it at all; but it is still a weight on her, and she feels it controls her life.

The rhythm of her days varies. She describes her days as "mostly chaos management". First thing in the morning, as soon as her alarm goes off, she checks emails, in case anything urgent has come in overnight. This does happen: she recently had a work-related email conversation with someone at 3 am. Her most productive time is in the morning, and for a while she had a successful strategy for research writing which was to block out regular time first thing in the morning to work on it, from 7.30 am onwards for a couple of hours. More recently, though, family commitments have got in the way of this.

She tries to find other ways to block out time for research writing, including booking mornings or afternoons in cabin spaces in outdoor settings to work in which have no internet access, to protect her from interruptions. But at times she has also found times to work interwoven with family activities, like writing during her child's swimming lessons, with the white noise of the water splashing providing a different kind of protection for her concentration.

During working hours, it is not unusual for her to have days which are back-to-back meetings. On those days, she has her email open all day and tries to deal with it quickly. However, if she is focusing on writing something – working on the student handbook, or writing a journal article – she closes the email down so that it does not distract her. She takes handwritten pencil notes in a Moleskine notebook at meetings, and makes notes about research on an iPad which she has with her always.

In the evening, she continues to work while her partner cooks tea. Even after going to bed she will talk about work with her partner, or read a journal article or an academic book, sometimes until midnight or beyond. She would usually check her emails again last thing at night – just in case.

In Diane's interviews, the constant pressure of emails is a strong theme running through all our discussions. Her days are framed by ways to try and hold back the ever-incoming tide, dealing with emails first thing in the morning, last thing at night, and in short breaks whenever she can throughout the day. It's clear, though, when she talks through her multiple research, teaching, and administrative commitments, that the volume of emails she deals with arises as a result of the many roles she plays in her working life and the many responsibilities that she has to deal with. She is constantly co-ordinating her activities with a very wide range of other people, both face-to-face in meetings and at a distance in her many collaborations, and so does not have the same scope that, for instance, Ian has for setting up a predictable rhythm for his working day which fits with his preferred working rhythms. Even when she did manage to carve out a predictable time for research writing, this only lasted for a period before family responsibilities started to eat into it. Nevertheless, she continues to work on blocking out time to focus on research writing, sometimes in quite creative ways. Her working day begins very early and extends to midnight or beyond. It is not surprising, therefore, that where Rebecca described her days as "hectic", Diane goes a step further in talking about her days as "chaos management". Having said that, she is perceived and rewarded as a highly successful academic in her department and in her field.

## Administrative writing and changing accountability demands

Don Robinson, a historian working in a research-intensive university, had a different kind of writing day later in September, when his department were busy getting ready for the teaching term. He had a key admin role in the department in relation to undergraduate teaching and learning, and all his writing tasks on this day related to meetings associated with this. He did check emails soon after he got up in the morning, but not on his phone and not the instant he awoke; instead he went to the PC in the study at home, to check whether anything urgent needed to be dealt with. He then came in to work to prepare for a teaching review meeting which he was chairing, on the basis of which he would produce a pro forma report for the faculty. The practical organisation of the meeting – circulation of agendas and papers, photocopying materials, room booking, email correspondence with people attending – had been done by the departmental administrator.

Preparation for the meeting meant going through reports he had previously drafted and using a highlighter pen to mark the parts that he wished to draw attention to during the meeting, including a response to the National Student Survey (NSS) results, the head of department's responses to the external examiners' reports, and an analysis of module evaluation questionnaires. The reports had been drafted in Word, a fairly straightforward task, adapting templates and models from previous years.

The meeting felt that the head of department's responses to the external examiners needed some reworking. These documents, which used to be for internal reference, were now required by the Quality Assurance Agency (QAA) to be made public to students. Where in previous years the focus of the responses had usually been on addressing any critical points in the reports, the meeting felt that the more public nature of the document now called for a more balanced approach which highlighted both the positive and negative points in the examiners' reports. After the meeting, Don spent the rest of the morning revising the responses accordingly. He took an analytic approach to this, using highlighter pens to mark-up positive and negative comments in the reports, and then cutting and pasting these into the letter grouped into themes with appropriate responses.

In the afternoon, he presented a report to the departmental meeting which he prepared in a similar way, but with less responsibility as he was not the chair. He did, however, have to engage with controversial discussions about students using mobile devices during lectures, and after the meeting sent emails to try to discover the university policy on this.

Don's day is notable in its almost entirely administratively focused nature, with no space for research at all. While this would not be a typical day for him, it does illustrate well the extensive writing demands associated with academic administrative responsibilities. Don engages in many writing tasks both to prepare for the meetings and immediately in response to them. Some of these tasks could be managed relatively straightforwardly, adapting models from previous years. But when aspects of the broader context changed, like the QAA requirements for making the documentation public, existing templates and models cannot be reproduced uncritically; change in regulation necessarily leads to change in documentation and to the requirement for the writer to learn to produce a certain genre in a different way. It is notable too that this requires more work; as well as the revised response letter being longer, the more public nature of the document serves both as a plan for future activity and as a public representation of the face of the department and the stakes are therefore higher, so Don takes extra care in putting it together. Throughout this book, we will be returning to issues around the requirements of accountability documentation such as this and the effects of it on people's everyday writing practices.

## Reactivity

James Gibson lectures in marketing at a teaching-intensive university. He normally checks his email on his iPad as soon as he gets up, at 6.30 am. He walks in to work and starts his working day at between 7.30 and 8 am. On the day discussed in the interview, he began the day sorting through emails, mostly dealing with PhD student issues such as fielding enquiries from applicants and arranging appointments, for a couple of hours. This was followed by a face-to-face supervision meeting between himself, a couple of other members of staff, and a PhD student, re-arranging her supervision schedule, followed up by a phone call to a colleague to discuss the complexities of this arrangement. He had previously shared an office with three others but had argued for a private office because of his role as research students' tutor where he carries out a lot of interviews and supervisions. A private office meant that "students can come in and unburden themselves of whatever is bothering them" without worrying about others listening in.

He had lunch with a publisher's representative, planning a potential textbook writing project. In the afternoon, he did some work for a journal which he is an associate editor for, processing articles which had been submitted, annotating template correspondence for reviewers and sending it off, and synthesising reviews of articles in order to make a recommendation to the editor in chief for a decision on publication. After that, he had blocked out a couple of hours for teaching preparation in which he checked that everything was available on the VLE that should be.

He went home just after 5 pm, ate, and then taught the first class of a new online module using Adobe Connect from his laptop at home: speaking with students through a headset, talking through the module information pack, responding to questions students sent in using text chat, and typing notes on assignment details which would remain available to the students after the session. This ensures that he has been very clear with the students about assignment expectations from the start of the course, particularly since the whole session was recorded. The class finished between 8.30 and 9.00 pm.

Again, James' working day is a long one, beginning with checking email at 6.30 am and going through to a teaching session ending at 9 pm. Working from home in the evening was facilitated by distance learning technologies which combine static and dynamic texts, talk, and video.

He finds it impossible to fit in much of what he calls "proactive" research time into these kinds of days. Most of his time is spent in "reactive" ways, responding to student and management requests within short timeframes and firefighting when problems arise. As a deliberate strategy, he sets up alternative kinds of days through the year which focus exclusively on pursuing his own research agenda by producing his own work and collaborating with PhD students and colleagues (we will discuss the strategies people use for constructing these kinds of boundaries more in Chapter 4). In the summer, he looks at his upcoming calendar for the year and blocks out as many days as he can to serve as research days, when he will spend the day at home writing and editing, without thinking about emails or things he has to do to deal with students.

## Weekly rhythm

Emma Kniveton is an early career lecturer in marketing at a research-intensive university, where she works comfortably in a quiet office of her own. She is still on probation and is concerned to ensure she produces the appropriate amount of publications to successfully get through probation. Her days during term time are structured around her teaching commitments. She teaches all day on

Thursdays, and earmarks Wednesdays for teaching preparation. She uses Monday for writing and research and deliberately making progress on things that are important to her. Tuesday is kept for research meetings and follow-ups. Friday depends on how she is feeling after the day before, and may include marking, admin, or writing.

Although Thursdays are teaching days between 11 am and 6 pm, she does do other kinds of writing as the day progresses. She comes in on the bus, using her commuting time to check email. On the Thursday in focus in the interview, before the teaching began she sent emails to confirm attendance at meetings, and to herself as a reminder of some changes to include in a research funding proposal she was working on for a colleague. She replied to a student sending apologies for the seminar, and multiple similar emails to students who had been unable to submit coursework the day before because the VLE had gone down.

Most of the teaching was working with MBA students, presenting on cases and discussing them. She got home between 8 and 8.30 pm, which was a typical return time for a Thursday.

---

Emma has a similar mixture of writing tasks to other participants in research-intensive universities, but she explicitly manages them by adopting a very disciplined approach to structuring her weeks. The idea of dedicating different days to different kinds of work and writing tasks is something that is mentioned by many of our participants, but which few achieve. Emma's success in organising her week in this way could be related in part to her background working in industry before joining academia, and in part to the importance she ascribes to achieving her probationary publication goals. Of course, the fact that her teaching is timetabled all together is an administrative reality that also makes this possible.

---

## Autonomy in writing, support from colleagues

Edward is a research associate working in a technical field on a short-term contract. His time is divided fairly evenly between software development research and academic writing. He is a productive writer who writes a lot of technical reports, funding bids, and articles for publication, with around half his time being spent on bids and articles. He is aware that there is pressure from the university for his group to publish articles regularly in particular kinds of journals, but he does not see this as a cause for concern, as his group are well over the target they are aiming for at the moment. In the year we interviewed him, he had published two articles with a colleague in high-ranking journals, had three under review, and had prepared around six funding bids. He feels he has a lot of autonomy in deciding what to write.

Despite this level of productivity, he describes writing as challenging. English is not his first language, and he feels his experience of writing is different from that of his colleagues who do speak English as their first language. However, he does not feel he is significantly disadvantaged by this overall, feeling it makes a 5–10% difference. One of his main concerns is in finding the appropriate synonym – "to write impressive words to express your research in a good way". He takes time when writing to search for the best words to use, and then asks his colleagues and his line manager to review sections of his work. At the moment, he uses Google to search for synonyms, but would like to see someone develop a technical solution to this, software which offers different options for sentences. The only training he has had specifically on writing is around writing research bids, which he described as being quite limited because the training was often specific to a given funding body.

Edward is an example of someone who draws on the resources around him in terms of work relationships in particular to support him in his writing. He is quite unusual amongst our participants in his description of his experience as being completely free to choose what to write. However, this experience of autonomy needs to be placed in the context of understanding that the kinds of texts he chooses to write are exactly the kinds of texts required by his university targets in any case. Already oriented towards technology, he finds technological solutions to some of his writing challenges and hopes that people are working on more sophisticated versions of these. But he also uses his colleagues and line manager as literacy brokers, drawing on their expertise as he develops his writing drafts.

### Never switching off

Charles Cooper is a senior lecturer in marketing at a research-intensive university. He works around 60 hours a week, including most weekends. He gets up between 5.30 and 6 am and checks emails on his phone straight away. He works on email on his laptop for half an hour or so, clearing around 15 "rubbish" ones, acting on two or three, and prioritising some to deal with during the day, and then goes for a run before dealing with his young children getting ready for school.

If he is coming in to the office, he aims to be at his desk at around 9 am, after dropping his children off at school. If he comes in at 9 am, he aims to leave at 6 pm and rarely socialises at work, though (unlike some) he leaves his office door mainly open in case students drop by. He tends to do his emails immediately after coming in; he feels he needs to get them dealt with as quickly as possible, although he feels he would be more productive if he did not turn emails on first thing, but says, "it goes against every grain in my body not to react to an email".

On a good day, he would aim to stop working on emails after about half an hour and then start working on research. He had 14 journal articles in preparation, at various stages of development, with a range of co-authors, working to a five-year plan.

On the day in focus discussed in the interview, he worked from home. In the morning, he made notes on some articles he had been tasked with reading for a co-authored paper for several hours. He collects pdfs of journal articles in Dropbox in folders organised by the writing project they relate to. He normally annotates them electronically using highlighting and notes, though if he has more time he might print them up and annotate them by hand. The first draft of the paper had received major revisions from a prestigious international journal, so he and his co-authors had had a whole-day meeting two weeks earlier to restructure the paper and divide tasks. Another meeting was planned on the next day, so his notes were in preparation for this.

He wrote around 30 emails in the afternoon, organising meetings with students and external examining work, and then went back to reading, this time in preparation for a change management project he is currently working on with a large external organisation. At 4.30 he spent a couple of hours preparing a PowerPoint presentation illustrating ways to approach change management in the organisation. He then carried out a literature search for more articles until 8.30 pm.

Charles is a successful academic, engaged in many projects and collaborating with a lot of people. We see in his account both the positive and negative aspects of this success. Like Diane, he works very long hours. This day was not unusual; it was common for him to begin work before 6 am and to finish at midnight or later, often spending the evenings on his laptop across the table from his wife who would be doing the same thing. Emails come in from students through the night, at 1, 2 or 3 am, and he has responded to them at that time if he happens to be up working, to get them out of the way quickly.

Again, like Diane, email looms large in his concerns. He finds emails overwhelming. He receives 60 to 80 a day, of which about 20 will be associated with some work and some thought. At the time of the interview, he had 14,000 emails in his inbox; at one point, his unread count alone was nearly 600.

He appreciates the flexibility of an academic job; in contrast to his previous consultancy career, no one needs to know where you are at all times. He uses this to work late, which can free up time during the day to spend with his family. The downside is that he never switches off. He wakes up every morning feeling sick with the pressure, and feels that he never gets any time to himself. He blames himself for this, saying that he finds it hard to prioritise and manage time effectively, but at the same time it is not clear how he could manage the many work activities and responsibilities he has in fewer hours than he does.

He described the day in focus in the interview as a rare day, when he got to spend a lot of time working on research. Most of his time was normally taken up doing other things, and when he does concentrate on research, he remains very aware that other people are always wanting something else from him.

---

### Control

Mark West lectured in marketing at a teaching-intensive university. He had a fairly long motorway commute, and his routine was to get into the office at 7 am to miss the traffic, and to spend the first two hours of the day working on his PhD (which he was doing at another university). This first two hours of the day was precious time for him, he felt he could get done in that time what it would have taken him six hours to do during the day.

At 9 am, he logged on to deal with the easy emails which might have come in overnight. Much of his work involved teaching in East Asia, and the time difference meant that overnight emails were common. On the day in focus in the interview, emails with the East Asian site were intensive as he was about to fly out there. He needed to remind people what was needed for the course he was delivering, and to prepare for a five-yearly revalidation by the government which was about to take place which required the production of extensive documentation. He then spent some time preparing for a plagiarism hearing, and emailing tutors who had not supplied grades for an upcoming academic board.

---

Mark's focus during the working day is, like that of the other academics in teaching-intensive universities, predominantly around teaching, both at the local university site in the UK and relating to his international teaching role in East Asia. Since he has a teaching leadership role, many of his tasks are related to this, particularly doing quality assurance work and chasing up documentation from other people. As division leader, he had a lot of administrative communications to engage in, especially related to quality assurance, saying "every day is a firefighting day, and you don't know what you're going to get". At the same time, he is working on a doctorate.

He has a range of strategies to manage these multiple responsibilities. He works long hours, getting to work after a long commute at 7 am, and using the hours before 9 am to focus on the doctorate work, setting a clear boundary between this research time and the "firefighting" role he takes on during the rest of the day. He keeps up with the pace of events by consistently writing notes in a notepad. He has a very structured approach to email, insisting on going to bed with an empty inbox, however late this might mean staying up. He was one of the few participants we interviewed who did not seem overwhelmed by the email load; this is helped by the fact that much of his email load comes in predictably overnight, enabling him to plan to catch up in this way day by day. Such conditions of synchronisation with collaborators and colleagues can have a significant effect on people's daily writing practices.

---

### The importance of finishing

Dolly Blue is a senior historian at a teaching-intensive university. He spent the day in focus working in his study at home, starting at 8.30 am working on a foreword to an exhibition catalogue which had both personal and professional resonance for him. He had 1,000 words to write, wrote the first draft in two hours and spent another hour polishing the piece, which he described as a fairly typical pattern for him.

On a home day of this kind, he would always leave the routine things like email until later. He spent a couple of hours on emails after lunch, and then started work on a book review in the afternoon. He had read the book a year ago, so started off by reminding himself of it. He had put sticky tags on useful quotes and started off by writing notes on the basis of these which gave him enough shape for the book review.

He finished the day marking some dissertations and finished at around 6 pm. He enjoys marking, feeling that it uses a different part of his brain from his research brain, and is an end-stopped task which he enjoys getting out of the way.

He described this day as a really good working day. He deliberately tries to construct days like this when he can, because he feels it is important to finish tasks to make the job bearable. To support this, he resists external demands of unreasonable deadlines and prioritises completing his own work. He tries to work at home two or three days a week.

---

Dolly was unusual in his explicit statement of the importance of finishing tasks (though we do see another version of this in Mark's commitment to emptying his inbox, above). Where many of our participants coped with the multiple demands of their work by setting boundaries in time, Dolly's strategy was to focus on setting boundaries around tasks and to include in each day tasks that could be finished that day. Where, as we have seen above, many of our participants used words like "firefighting", "chaos" and "pressure" to talk about the multiple writing demands they faced, Dolly explicitly articulated resistance to external demands that he perceived as being unreasonable and prioritised work that he was committed to personally. We should not overlook his institutional position and status in explaining this. Where Emma, for instance, was concerned to get through her probation requirements, and Charles was worried about making progress in his career, Dolly was well-established with professorial status. At the same time, he had been in academia for long enough to see and be sceptical about many of the increased demands related to managerialism and accountability.

## Conclusion

These vignettes have introduced a sample of our research participants, the different demands they face in their writing days and the variety of strategies they use to respond to these. We have seen a range of experiences, from those who feel pressured and overwhelmed to a smaller number whose strategies and positions provide them with a sense of control. We have seen the effects of some of the trends in higher education discussed in earlier chapters on the realities of people's lives: increased managerialism in universities, particularly around REF and other accountability strategies; digitisation supporting collaborative communication and innovative teaching but also leading to digital overload, particularly around email; and the material constraints and possibilities of the particular configurations of space, time, and resources people are working within. In the following chapters, we explore many of these themes in more detail, beginning with a focus on academic writing practices in time and space.

# 4

# ACADEMICS WRITING IN SPACE AND TIME

## Introduction

As we argued in Chapter 1, to approach literacies from a socio-material practice perspective entails recognising the embeddedness of literacy practices in social contexts, and particularly in space and time. The organisation of time and space at work has long been a topic of interest for research (see Taylor & Spicer, 2007; Van Marrewijk & Yanow, 2010; Dale & Burrell, 2007). In most workplaces, employees are tied to particular places and times as conditions of their work, and in many occupations, attendance is strictly enforced. Academics are unusual as professional workers in that, in most (though not all) institutions, they have a degree of autonomy in choosing where and when they will work. As long as the teaching is delivered, the research carried out, the admin tasks completed, and the email answered in relatively good time, there is minimal checking-in or checking-out of the office, and few set office hours in most academic jobs. Such privileged control over the pace and place of working has traditionally been a highly valued part of the academic role.

In the previous chapter, we saw examples of the kinds of deliberate choices academics make about where and when to write. Most of our participants described such spatial and temporal choices, some expressing very strong personal preferences. And yet, many of our participants expressed a sense of *lacking* autonomy over their working lives. This chapter will explore this apparent paradox through examining the spaces and times of academics' workplace writing, the choices academics make in their writing locations, and the external factors which constrain those choices.

Social geographers and philosophers have shown how space and time are socially constructed, fluid, and performed in everyday practices, an approach which is compatible with our socio-material and practice-oriented perspective on academics' writing practices. May and Thrift (2003) make a convincing argument for treating time/space as indivisible aspects of experience. They build on Massey's (1994) work on the uneven geographies of practice, which shows how people's perspective on and social practices around mobility and flows in space are patterned by existing power relationships. Some social groups have the power to initiate flows and movement, while others are subject to such flows (see also Castells, 2010, on the space of flows). In this chapter, we draw on such approaches to show how academics inhabit, help create, and move around in the spaces and times available to them, developing strategies to manage the tensions and demands of their working lives. In particular, we will highlight the importance of the construction of boundaries in space and time, identifying where challenges to these boundaries originate (see discussions of blurred boundaries in Tuck, 2018b), and how those challenges are experienced and negotiated by academics in their writing choices.

## Space

Many different groups of people inhabit and use a university campus. Research on the material spaces of education (e.g. Nespor, 2014; Lawn & Grosvener, 2005; Temple, 2014) shows that the different groups who inhabit these spaces (such as academics, students, and administrators) have different perceptions of them, having different uses for them and moving through them in different ways. Students' movements through and perceptions of campus space are very different from academics', although the dimensions they identify are similar (see Liao et al., 2013).

Lefebvre's (1991) distinction between spaces as designed, perceived, and lived allows for the possibility of different perspectives on space, and helps clarify the powerful symbolic aspects of space that are present in any university environment. Universities are "designed spaces" and maintenance and development of the university estate are important though often invisible strands of management (Temple & Barnett, 2007). Universities develop "masterplans" for their use of space which link closely to their financial and strategic plans for upcoming years. These strategic and space masterplans reflect the contemporary influences of marketisation, digitisation, and internationalisation which we have already discussed. The resulting spaces are corporate and outward-facing and the working practices of academics are only one among many factors which influence institutional decision-making in this area.

The writing that academics do as professionals is a central part of their contractual requirements, and universities do provide academics with spaces in which to work. These are both physical office-spaces, but also protected time in the form of sabbatical leave and lighter teaching and administrative loads for probationary staff. But spaces also need to be provided for different kinds of teaching (large or small groups, computer labs, performance arts), for different kinds of research (desk-based, archival, specialised laboratories with particular equipment, etc.), for student accommodation (now one of the ways in which universities market themselves) and for associated facilities. A great deal of importance is currently placed by university estates planners on providing a welcoming learning environment for students and prospective visiting students. We did come across some examples where academics had been consulted about the design of their working environment, but this was not common practice.

All of the academics we worked with closely had offices at, and provided by, the university. Most of them had individual offices (a few were shared). And yet, very few of them worked exclusively in these offices. Don, a historian, is fairly typical in this respect, explaining that: "Any serious writing for research, I would basically do at home in my study. The writing which has more to do with administration, I would tend to do in the office." While Don's perspective is fairly neutral emotionally, others expressed stronger positions. Louis, a historian, explained that "I do not use the office for writing because that is too disruptive and despairing. I write either in libraries or in cafés". Rebecca, another historian, stated in stronger terms:

> I would say that of all the places that I would use for writing, anywhere in the university is a long way down the list. That's only in extremis would I write within the university, on the campus, and the bottom of the places that I would use on campus is my office.

It was therefore common for many of our participants to carry out a certain amount of their work at home. Usually, home was described as being a better place than the office for focused writing, because it was a space where people could avoid interruptions. As Will, a mathematician, explains:

> I tend to do a lot of my writing and initiating things, documents, at home. That is because the department is somewhere I can come and I can be interrupted ... In other words, it's not a good place to write, to just settle down and start writing.

Personal circumstances did affect this choice, though. Alan, a mathematician, was more likely to use travelling time to write than to work at home, because of his caring responsibilities: "If I need to write, I can write on the train. At home, well, my daughter is four, so it's hard to write when she's awake." Even where caregiving responsibilities are less intense, working at home can have its distractions. James, a marketing academic, explained that:

> In the past I've struggled to work from home, partly because my former laptop was a bit long in the tooth, partly because we have a cat who constantly – if I'm home then obviously I'm there to pay attention to

him. There are other activities of course that happen at home, things like laundry and preparing dinner and so on and so forth that get in the way of real focus.

He, too, though, found that working in the office was accompanied by frequent interruptions. There are therefore broader questions about equality which are raised around people's differential levels of access to working spaces which support different kinds of writing. This was highlighted by the more restricted (see Figure 4.1) and often shared office facilities offered by

FIGURE 4.1 Some office spaces were very restricted

less well-resourced universities and occupied by administrative staff who are in less privileged spaces in the academy.

Even where a person worked predominantly in one room, they made choices about the spaces they were working in. For example, Verity and Clara, senior academics in history, had both set up different desks for different types of work. Clara had set up one desk like a "work space" for "looking at spreadsheets and stuff like that", and another for her research writing – which she described as "the luxury bit" – with more tactile things around it, in a more restful space. Verity had one desk with a computer – "my word processing desk" – and another one facing the window and trees, where she would draft and scribble with a pen and paper until she felt ready to go onto the computer. "Some of my most agonising writing experiences take place at this wooden desk, and then go to that white desk and, hopefully, it's all a bit easier transferring it onto the screen." Note that the furniture, and the physical materials that make up the buildings as well as layout and views from windows, affect choices and comfort; and note the emotional weight in the descriptions of the "luxury bit" and the "agonising writing".

Many people described working in public spaces, making use of the "fuzzy" in-between (neither work nor personal) times of travelling to and from work or visiting other colleagues and work locations. Cafés were mentioned by some, like Louis above; Patricia, an early career marketing academic, said, "I love the coffee shops in town ... sometimes I go and work there when I really think that I need to go somewhere completely different ... I don't mind the background noise or anything if I work". Public transport was another space which was protected from interruptions; as Robert, a mathematician, explained, "Where do I write that? Trains are fantastic ... because you have two or three hours where, going down to London, nobody can irritate you".

Some people claimed to be able to write anywhere, regardless of the physical conditions, so long as they could do so uninterrupted. Some actively preferred to think on the move, which could offer unexpected moments of creativity. Will, mentioned above, said that when writing lectures:

> Monday morning, I will think a bit more carefully about the flow of things I am going to say and how I will explain some things. I will often do that on the way in. When I am travelling or walking on the street. It is kind of loading it up so that when I am actually in the lecture I have been thinking about it and it flows hopefully.

This kind of mobile working is not without its constraints (power sources and internet connections especially when flying; the need to carry equipment and papers around) but is greatly facilitated by the development of mobile digital devices.

For the majority of our participants, electronic resources and repositories had replaced the physical books and journals that they used to consult, and as a result, they rarely visited a library. Libraries and archives were discussed as spaces for work by some, however, especially the historians we interviewed. This was both for practical reasons – access to original documents – but also aesthetic ones; as Dolly Blue told us, "What idiot would look at a screen for hours on end when you can be in a beautiful library flicking through stuff?" Diane described the library as having

> a weight in the air … I feel the intensity of that trying to be quiet, because it's not quiet, but trying to be quiet, is enough for me to be able to sometimes step into writing, when I'm procrastinating and avoiding.

The aesthetic and sensory aspects of the spaces in which people were writing proved to be surprisingly important. Charles, for instance, explained to us that he would really prefer to be outside, so whenever he could manage it, he would take himself to a café with views over fields and hills, working on his Mac which had an intuitive and ergonomic setup and a keyboard he found much more pleasant than his office machine. He explained, "I find the physicality of the place I'm working very important; I work faster, and quicker, and more efficiently". Figure 4.2 shows the desk of one of our participants who found it helpful to write with a pleasant view out onto a green space.

The spatial fabric of university life is constantly changing. In all three of our focal universities, spatial disruption was a fact of life, a by-product of the

FIGURE 4.2 Views of green space and light help this writer

expanding higher education industry (see Figure 4.3). People were moved around as buildings were refurbished or rebuilt. In our teaching-intensive institution, in particular, several of our participants moved office over the course of the project – some more than once. Ian, a maths lecturer, describes his precarious working space:

> I'm sharing at the moment with a colleague who's based in London and he's on research leave, very kindly offered me the use of his office. And so I've parked myself with some of the boxes of books that I was able to salvage before the contents of my room were parcelled up and sent off to a warehouse.

Elizabeth, working at the teaching-intensive university, used to come in early and get writing done in her single office but had recently been moved into shared temporary accommodation, an unrefurbished space which she found uncomfortable to be in. She now went in only when she was teaching: "until they sort our offices out, there's no way you can do any work in that place". Such temporary and disrupted spaces are not conducive to concentrated writing for extended periods without interruption. Even changing the direction of someone's office desk could have an impact. When Diane moved offices and found herself facing in the opposite direction, she found it took three months to feel she was able to write again, because the move and the sense of facing the other way were "massively disruptive" for her.

Like the middle-manager clinicians discussed by Ainsworth et al. (2009), having a certain degree of autonomy and the ability to move freely while getting work done was indeed, therefore, valued by our academic participants,

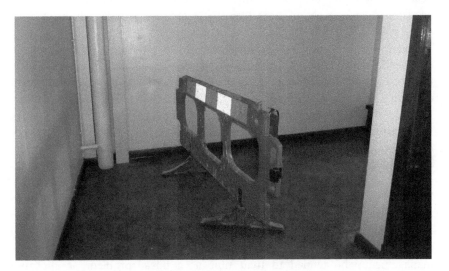

FIGURE 4.3 Building works and refurbishments were common disruptions

both for practical reasons (avoiding interruptions) and for reasons which related to their own aesthetic and sensory experiences of their spaces of work.

## Time

Working people in many industries report an experience of "time squeeze" (Southerton, 2003). This resonates with the accounts of our participants. Hochschild's (1997) classic account of the "time bind" in the workplace shows how increasing efficiency through fragmenting and reorganising time leads to experiences of time pressure and anxiety. Widerberg (2006) identifies factors contributing to experiences of time pressure for engineers and teachers, including multiple conflicting expectations and demands, requirements that tasks be done quickly, unlimited possibilities for creativity and exploration around technical issues, and tasks extending between home and work. Teachers were particularly strained by the need to be regularly "on display" and so masked their feelings of tiredness and pressure, an experience shared by teaching academics. O'Carroll (2008) identifies similar tensions between fast-paced productivity and time for creativity and development in the IT industry, fitting different kinds of work into "fuzzy gaps" in the day leading to an experience of never quite being "not working", exacerbated by constant switching to monitor "micro-tasks" such as email (on which, more later). Time for reflection and creativity is necessary for the production of tangible outputs such as computer code and reports, but is hard to measure and therefore hard to value.

In Chapter 1, we discussed the pressures academics experience from managerialist accountability systems designed to heighten productivity in publication. These pressures have a strong temporal dimension, with research on academics' experiences of time identifying tensions particularly around the pace of work.

Several researchers have explored the diversity in the ways academics experience time, reinforcing a perspective that rejects a linear "clock time" perspective and instead seeks to understand time as multiple, dynamic, and changing (Lingard & Thompson, 2017). Ylijoki and Mäntylä (2003) identi-fied four different time perspectives which academics experience. "Scheduled time" associated with externally imposed and controlled timetables was perceived both as constraining, and as taking place at a pace continually accelerated by increasing numbers of externally imposed obligations at shorter and shorter timescales. In contrast, research work would ideally be characterised by "timeless time", immersion in the task at hand, deep reflection, and critical thinking; but this was described more as a hope or ideal than a reality, given the dominance of "scheduled time". Like O'Carroll's (2008) IT workers, such complexities of temporal experience could not easily be engaged with by management who tended to treat time as a linear problem of allocation and productivity, focusing on concrete outputs, rather than recognising the complex lived reality of academics' multiple temporal challenges. Many of the academics Ylijoki and Mäntylä  worked with were also working on short-term and insecure contracts, a "contracted time" which generated anxiety and a short-term focus on evaluation and survival. "Personal time", with family or in leisure activity, was described as highly threatened, both by "scheduled time" and "timeless time".

These four perspectives on time were all apparent in the experiences described by the academics in our study and link to the strategies they explained to us as they try to optimise conditions for their writing – searching for uninterrupted space, spaces they can control, and making use of the "in-between" spaces of travelling and personal time.

Lefebvre (1991) identifies pace, intensity, rhythm, and routine as significant aspects of how time is experienced. These are the points at which collective and individual times intersect and we documented many in our data. Some markers of pace and rhythm for individual academics' writing tasks are externally set deadlines. These may be recurrent ones such as yearly exam boards, or one-off publisher's deadlines agreed by contract. Where an individual is subject to several such deadlines, they have to deal with multiple overlaid timescales in prioritising their writing work.

Other determinants of pace and rhythm in writing entangle the writer in a different way since certain writing tasks (e.g. preparing for and following up on a meeting) are integral to the logic of the event (there is no point in preparing after the meeting has taken place). The social actions of meeting and making decisions, compel priority to be given to the writing that needs to be done to record these even if, in the wider scheme of things, there is more significant writing to be done. In other words, "urgency" and "importance" are not at all the same thing. If there are too many "urgent" tasks, an individual ends up spending all their time doing these and never prioritises the really important writing that needs to be done.

In a similar way, Smith (2015) identifies on the basis of ethnographic research with Czech academics three distinct temporal regimes governing the knowledge production of academics which combine and intersect with each other in often problematic ways: individualised career time, based on shared "scripts" of what constitutes an appropriate career development trajectory; the objective-driven, emergent, precarious, and short-term time of collaborative projects; and the imagined timelessness of the disciplinary community.

Müller (2014) identifies a similar diversity of perspectives, identifying pace, fragmentation, and the pressure to always be one step ahead as the tangible temporal experiences of problematic trends in academia. The postdoctoral researchers Müller interviewed manage such tensions through behaviours characterised by "anticipatory acceleration", which aim to tame future uncertainties by framing academic work as an international metrics-based competition. The researchers anxiously heighten the pace at which they write academic papers in order to gain enough academic capital to move into a secure position – "an increase of countable academic output per pre-defined unit of time" (see Introduction section, para. 4). Müller has concerns about how this perspective affects the production of knowledge, decreasing the likelihood such scholars will work on riskier, more complex research problems where papers are not guaranteed and developing a competitive, individualised, and instrumental perspective rather than seeing research as a collective and collegial mission.

Our participants' stories reflect these accounts. Lack of adequate time to focus on writing was one of their greatest difficulties. Ian told us his most significant challenge was

> Time ... It's having a period of a few weeks or something like that, where you don't have to think of another thing. It's really disruptive to your concentration to have to go back and do three hours one day on something [else] ... It's clear that there are lots and lots of things which get in the way.

The choices people made about working space described above were largely designed to minimise these interruptions, these "things which get in the way", reflecting the distinction between "scheduled" and "timeless" time.

But we can also identify another characteristic time experience: "fragmented time". We have already described the multitude of demands faced by the academics who participated in this project, and this led to an experience of work time as being increasingly disjointed. When working on campus, people were subject to a range of physical interruptions – people arriving at the office, whether students or colleagues, with questions or tasks which changed their focus of the task they were working on and brought in new issues. As Will told us, "You think, 'I've got two hours. I'm going to get something done', and then it just takes one knock on the door to interrupt that".

Having said that, fragmentation could also have positive effects, reflecting O'Carroll's (2008) identification of work getting done in "fuzzy gaps" between other tasks. Gareth, a mathematician, said that

> The opportunity to forward-think for research happens in weird gaps in my life rather than work-time, if I'm honest ... This morning, I suddenly had – something I'd just read on an email from someone on collaboration. Suddenly, I was thinking about that; "Oh, I can use that to solve a problem somewhere else". Those types of things, they fit in little gaps.

From a broader perspective looking at longer timescales, time in academic life is charted and controlled in various ways, sliced up into blocks of various sizes (sessions, modules, terms, years), producing a certain kind of time and rhythm. The undergraduate teaching year is often dominant; Nespor (2007) shows how undergraduate students use the organisations and representations of time in undergraduate programmes to navigate their way through the university. But this is only one of the many timescales (Lemke, 2000) academics live within and orient towards. The immediate timescales of each academic year are very different from the seven-year REF cycle, or the long and unpredictable timeframes associated with the publication of journal articles or books.

The timescales of tasks required by university and departmental administrators were often of the order of days and weeks. Teaching and marking, again, were on immediate timescales with hard deadlines. Lectures have to be written for the day they are to be taught. Marking deadlines are very tightly enforced by institutions concerned about their National Student Survey (NSS) scores. Other kinds of writing associated with teaching were also subject to external deadlines and writing these took up time, too. David, a mathematician, explained that the demands of the quality assurance process had led to him being engaged recently in:

> Just writing – making sure that the documentation is correct ... See what's in the course handbooks, all have proper descriptions and agree with each other ... I can see the point of it but ... it takes on its own momentum ... the university, the people in charge of these things always seem to insist on far too much ... there's no understanding of the amount of time these things take and the fact that it's yet another demand on your time.

The timescales of these kinds of demands were in tension with the timescales of scholarly writing which are often much longer, and also more fluid. People struggled to prioritise scholarly writing when facing these more immediate demands, despite the fact that promotion and academic esteem relate very directly to productivity in research writing (supporting the account given by Nygaard, 2017). As Connor, a head of department in history at the teaching-intensive university, explained, there is a constant tension between tasks which needed to be prioritised by time or by significance:

> The course leader's annual report is, to my mind, not a particularly important task, but it has to be done every year by a certain date ... it's not that significant, but teaching materials, they are the most important, because that's the main work that we do. Of course, writing a whole range of research-type writings is important.

But research-related writing, important though it is, rarely has the specific deadlines that teaching and administrative reports do.

Managing these conflicting timescales was a real challenge. In contrast to our methodological principle of symmetry (Pardoe, 2000), our participants often distinguished between work they valued and felt was central, designated by terms like "real", "actual", "substantial" or "serious" work, which they struggled to find time for, and "all the other stuff", often the many kinds of routine "maintenance" writing associated with keeping the university running, which squeezed out the "real" work. Juliette said that,

> There are periods that I can't get any substantial writing done at all, because there's just too much admin, and teaching, and other things going on that I don't ... I'm the type of person who needs a block to do it. I can't do half an hour in-between a meeting. It just doesn't work for me, because I need to think a lot while I write.

Verity told us that "the actual creative work, of writing, I do at home". Alan distinguished between "useful and exciting" writing – writing you really want to do – and "non-exciting" writing, such as emails and marking. Jen told us that she didn't do "serious" writing in the office, that would be done at home.

In terms of time, as discussed above, the more highly valued writing work characterised in this way often required time for reflection that could not easily be factored in. Clara, who was the head of a history department, identified the pace of academic life as a problem for the quality of thinking:

> Writing is a slow process. Things like REF don't necessarily factor in that writing is a form of thinking. As you write, you process and you reflect and you think and arguably we need to speed all that up because we now have these deadlines and these targets ... that need to speed up, you just kind of short circuit somewhere along the line the thinking and reflection process.

In addition to the problem of competing timescales, several of our participants reported that the dominant rhythms of the university year were changing, leaving less and less time protected from immediate demands. Blocks of time which used to be devoted to research and research-related writing, such as the summer or other vacations, were encroached upon by internationalisation, by degree programmes running on non-standard timescales, and by increased demands around marking and feedback. Diane told us, for instance, "There's not a block where you can say I'm doing writing. We used to have the summer. But things like overseas partners, it massively intrudes on everything". Greater student numbers and expectations for lengthier feedback on assessed work increase the time spent marking, which can also affect these annual rhythms. Rebecca, a historian, said, "It used to be the case that I could get some [research writing] done during Christmas and Easter vacations. Increasingly less so. That's taken up by marking really".

Interacting with the managerialist pressures (Shepherd, 2018) shaping academics' temporal experience are the temporal effects of digital technology.

This has rapidly become the predominant way in which the majority of academics' work is done and organised (Goodfellow & Lea, 2013), and huge volumes of communication flow into academics' lives by digital means. Digital devices can change temporal practices in different ways, as Gourlay (2014) shows: slowing things down (through technology failure or information overload), speeding things up (leaving some struggling to keep up with new technologies), intruding into established temporalities through constant entanglement with devices, or sequencing and focusing embodied action. Hassan (2003) argues that a major shift has taken place from the "clock time" of the last century's industrial workplaces to a "network time" associated with both digital technologies which enable the compression of time and the neoliberal organisation of knowledge production, driven by a logic of competition, commerce, and instrumentality. Knowledge, as we saw in the first chapter, becomes seen as a commodity to be exchanged in a marketplace rather than a shared social good. Individuals have to act fast and make speedy decisions to maximise their job market chances, and this is reflected both in the wider workplace and in universities. Indeed, Pels (2003) argues that a key way in which universities are losing their distinctiveness is by adopting the rhythms of politics and of the business world, rather than privileging the traditionally longer timescales of academia. (We discuss the impact of digital technologies more fully in Chapter 6.)

Menzies and Newson (2007), mapping out changes in the Canadian university sector, also see the globally wired university as part of the neoliberal global economy. They argue that the pursuit of "efficiency through time-compression" is associated with a change in the temporality of universities which resonates throughout academics' daily routines and rhythms, associated with both increased levels of stress and changes in how knowledge is produced in universities. The managerialist approach to accountability and the introduction of business languages and strategies they describe are familiar (Shepherd, 2018); they argue that information and communications technologies make it possible for universities to function as "permeable, multi-purpose, networked knowledge businesses" (and see Castells, 2010, on the impact of the shift to a network society). The important thing in terms of the current focus is their identification of the impact of this on knowledge production, when most of academics' interactions take place via email, leaving little space for deep reflection or collaborative knowledge creation. They claim that under these conditions, technology facilitates multitasking, skim-reading, and an individualised focus on the production of papers at a rapid pace, losing the sense of the university as a "social space-time of shared learning and knowing" which supports deep reflection and critical thinking.

We have already discussed the fragmentation of temporal experience caused by multiple interruptions. Digital technologies further augment this fragmentation. Virtual spaces afford simultaneous access to multiple layers of work and time. Even when away from the office and protected from directly co-present interruptions, email and the ubiquitous digital devices carried by nearly all of our participants opened them up to the potential for the tasks they engaged in to be constantly interrupted by other requests. As Gareth told us,

> You tend to not want to fire up the laptop or something and have it on your knee, but the iPad, I tend to be watching TV, looking at various news bits on there, but then emails are coming in and out and you're doing all of those things as well.

It was very common in our data for people to check their email on a phone or tablet right at the start of the day, often on waking, and email engagement could extend until late at night. Gareth told us, too, that

> I've got a few colleagues who, like me, work too hard who – we all just create each other even more emails. We complain about being busy but then send an email to each other and start a communication at half-eleven at night.

Oztok et al. (2014) discuss how virtual learning environments and email open up "always on" channels of communication between teachers and students. When teachers' and students' timeframes clash – when a student emails at 2 am, for instance, and a teacher perceives this as requiring a speedy response – this can exacerbate the sense of always-on time pressure.

## Strategies

Our research participants adopted a range of concrete temporal and spatial strategies to deal with these challenges. All of these could be interpreted as setting boundaries around particular, valued kinds of work, in different ways, often making choices around their spaces of work in order to protect a period of time; one example of the integrated nature of the experience of times and spaces, as argued by May and Thrift (2003) and others.

People tried to set different times for different types of work. For some, this was done in a rhythmic, routined way, associating particular times of the day regularly with particular types of work, or keeping disruptive activities like checking email routinely out of particular times of day. Ian, for instance, kept late afternoons and evenings for what he counted as "serious" writing, which he found easier at that time of day. Less serious writing, which he glossed as "emails and so on", was kept to other times of day. Sean, a historian, told us he had made a deliberate decision to stop checking emails at the weekend and on holidays when he realised "I had allowed that to intrude". Rory, in marketing, where possible, arranged his teaching into blocks which gave him some days free to dedicate to research, which he tended to do at home, where he had more space to think.

Others would use their calendar to block out chunks of time for particular tasks, but this could be at different times of day. As one of the marketing academics, Mark, told us,

> When I write I tend to look for a block of hours, minimum I would suggest two or three hours, which I can actually do something and minimise interruptions. That can of course happen in the office, although less likely in many ways these days. So I can do it at home quite often. So that's the way I tend to organise my time.

Ella, another marketing academic who was working towards a doctorate in education, found that while for most of her working day she was happy to work in the office and swap between small chunks of different activities, for writing her thesis she needed to commit whole days to it regularly and go off to a quiet zone in the library to enable her to work without distractions and interruptions.

However, this kind of time-blocking was dependent on having a certain amount of control over one's time. Pippa, who had a wide range of administrative and managerial responsibilities in a large Management School, understood the value of planning to write for two hours a day but found this impossible given the responsibilities she faced each day, and instead she would "binge write", working very long hours in the run-up to a deadline to get research writing done.

Holly, an administrator who worked part-time, was very aware of the need to protect her non-work time, even expressing this using the word "boundary" as a verb: "I really try to boundary." She used a range of conscious strategies to achieve this, including not having the virtual private network on her computer at home, and only accessing emails via webmail. Despite her conscious commitment to this strategy, though, she still found these boundaries challenged. For instance, she sometimes found herself working on her non-work days when she needed to get in touch with people who were only themselves available at that time.

Another way of setting boundaries was to organize and commit to non-work-related activities. Pippa, a senior academic in marketing, committed to non-work activities on certain evenings, such as swimming sessions, deliberately to stop herself working all the time.

Setting boundaries around work was not enough to address the demands faced by some people, who took a different approach of extending the times and spaces when they engaged in work-related writing. Rather than setting and maintaining boundaries, this strategy extended the time of writing across boundaries – boundaries between day and night; home and work; personal and public; and sometimes boundaries between different types of work, too.

Asked how many hours a week he worked, David explained that,

> Probably like most university members of staff, you do your teaching and admin. That takes up most of the time and the research is done in your spare time so I hate to think how many hours. Probably, I'd say about 65 a week, something like that ... You start work before you come in and you're also working in the evenings and then probably working Sundays as well.

Charles told us,

> I do work evenings, and I do work weekends sometimes. Research takes me a long time ... I get emails from students all the way through ... If you're up and working at 1, 2, 3 in the morning or you're up anyway, it's tempting just to try and action it just then with a quick fire response.

Here, boundaries between work time and non-work time, between research and teaching work, and between home and work are all being breached in the interest of responding to emails from students and getting them dealt with as quickly as possible – another kind of strategy for the pressures of multiple demands.

Collin was aware of the strategy of setting boundaries but found it hard to implement, saying, "I'm not very self-disciplined as I think some people are". He described himself as "a cause of some despair, probably, at home" because he would often be working long hours at home – through to 10 pm or later – whether on his own writing or in response to tight deadlines at work, because "it's easier to do that work at 9 pm than to feel I will have time in the working day, when I might, but I might be interrupted".

Some of our participants saw this flexibility as a positive aspect of their work. Richard explained that after several hours of teaching in a day, he needed some time to relax before he could concentrate on work again; working from home afforded him the possibility to do this. While he worked "Saturday, Sunday or sometimes evening as well", he feels this makes his life easier; "working only at the office would be difficult really".

This extension of work time was not just true of the academics we interviewed; some of the administrators also extended their working hours at busy times. Kirsty, an undergraduate administrator in a maths department, found that during exam period, her busiest time, she would work evenings and weekends and would sometimes be on email at 11 pm. Steve, an administrator with responsibilities for producing key REF documentation, frequently worked 10–12 hour days for the 18 months around the REF period. However, it was more common for the administrative staff to have much clearer boundaries than the academic staff. For example, Sheena, another administrator in a maths department, did not check emails or work outside of her set hours and did not use her work email for personal matters.

Even for those people who actively do set boundaries in space and time, these boundaries were constantly being challenged. The most significant source of these challenges was in the constant inflow of digital communication. While physical interruptions could be avoided by moving away from the office, digital interruptions were harder to manage. Some participants did make a conscious choice to avoid these interruptions – by switching off mobile phones, putting them in drawers, or not installing email programmes on them in the first place. But where people did not have explicit strategies for managing digital interruptions, these were a significant presence in their working lives. Boundaries are fragile to construct and easy to breach, and constant maintenance work goes on around them.

Clearly, this extension of the time spent on all kinds of work writing practices could lead to problems with work–life balance and potentially to exhaustion, which is not conducive to creative or innovative work. This is not, of course, an issue solely for academics. Southerton (2003) writes about an increased sense of being "harried", rushed, and living in haste, which is associated with increased "flexibilisation" of working times and spaces, as we move from a default 9–5 working pattern to a 24-hour society. While the pressures experienced by his participants are different from those of ours – his participants are keeping up with the Joneses socially, ours are keeping up with their publication profile – the sources of this sense of harriedness are familiar: "'harriedness' resulted from incompatibility between the volume of tasks allocated within time frames and the temporal (and necessarily spatial) coordination of networks" (Southerton, 2003, p. 15). The strategies Southerton's participants adopted to address this harriedness are similar to some of those described by our participants, including adopting fixed socio-temporal routines, and using co-ordinating devices like mobile phones (or email in the case of our academics). However, he describes all of these strategies as "individual responses to a collective problem" (p. 22). He argues that part of the contribution to this harriedness is "collective deroutinisation", when regular social routines which used to guide the completion of tasks disappear, in a similar way to how the traditional routines and rhythms of the academic year have come under pressure as described above.

## Conclusion

Institutional priorities and the design of academic spaces are often in tension with the needs of those working in them. Academics manage conflicting pressures by setting boundaries in space and time to protect highly valued knowledge-creation work. As discussed above, many participants attempted a spatial bounding of "serious" (scholarly and research writing) work which is only ever done at home, combined with the temporal bounding of administrative tasks like email responding which is done during "office hours" of nine to five.

When the autonomy to set these boundaries is challenged, and when the boundaries are encroached upon, this causes problems. Changes around expectations in communication, often left implicit, have exacerbated these issues.

Individuals need to have ways to protect the practices necessary for the kinds of writing that are of the greatest import and value to them as well as to their institutions. This would include thinking through explicitly how to create and manage boundaries; managing interruptions; and protecting autonomy and choice. Institutions need to recognise this; understand the challenges of dealing with so many demands on different timescales; design spaces to meet academics' needs as well as students'; and develop explicit, negotiated statements about what is reasonable: around working time, email communication, availability. A key role of universities could be to create cultures that protect and nurture the writing and writers that are so central to institutional success.

# 5

# DISCIPLINES, GENRES, AND WRITING

This chapter turns to how academics experience and describe their disciplinary identities, and how this shapes their writing practices. It focuses on the concepts of discipline and genre and how these are experienced by the academics in our study. It discusses how writing practices are distributed across areas of knowledge production, and how they are changing. We deal with discipline-based ideas about knowledge, and how it is created, and what forms of knowledge are valued, including the satisfactions and frustrations of concerns with impact.

We draw attention to what is described as being of particular value in the writing of selected disciplines – how these different disciplines construct knowledge. Such differences do not always fit well with the implicit understandings of a managerialist approach to the university, nor with the accountability systems such as research assessment structures introduced by central government. Tensions between these notions play out in concrete terms in our participants' writing practices, in the decisions they make about what kinds of texts to write, and also in the frustrations they feel about what kinds of texts they have to write.

## Disciplines

We designed the project to work with individuals with contrasting disciplinary backgrounds, investigating how disciplinary location interplayed with their institutional setting and their academic biography in their everyday workplace writing practices. Our initial intention was to work with people from one science, one humanities, and one professional or applied discipline in order to represent a range of perspectives. There was also the practical motivation of focusing on subjects which were taught in the three universities we planned to work in. We selected mathematics, history, and marketing to represent these different perspectives. However, it rapidly became clear that such an apparently neat distinction was more complicated in real life, reinforcing the idea of the complexity of disciplinary identification discussed in Chapter 2. The academics we worked with saw their disciplinary identities in very different ways. While one or two people unproblematically described themselves as, for instance, "a historian" or "a mathematician", the majority of our participants explained carefully that they were not located in their disciplines in a straightforward manner, or that they described their disciplines differently for different audiences, and that their intellectual biography had moved them in and out of different disciplines. Some of our participants had a PhD in one subject but were now working in another, which complicated their understandings of their disciplinary "home".

In addition, disciplines did not always map easily onto departments and each university had a different breakdown of departments and disciplines. For example, one of the universities we worked with did not have academic departments devoted to single disciplines, but instead had multi-disciplinary schools with names such as "Humanities and social sciences", within which history sat alongside subjects like criminology and design. Likewise, the discipline of mathematics was found, in some cases, within schools of physical sciences and in others in its own school. In some cases, mathematics was combined with statistics within one department, while in others, the "mathematical sciences" such as statistics, probability, pure maths, and applied maths were listed separately.

A further issue worth mentioning in attempting to examine writing practices within and across disciplines is that the disciplines we selected were not necessarily representative of science, humanities, or professional practice disciplines. Disciplinary communities are not monolithic and no single representative discipline encapsulates the essence of sciences, humanities, or professional practice. One might argue, for example, that core features of science disciplines are that they tend to employ quantitative methods to study natural phenomena and tend to be experimental and predictive. However, mathematics, particularly at the pure end of the continuum, does not fit neatly into this paradigm. Pure mathematicians may not be particularly concerned with predicting or explaining natural phenomena, but instead focus on the study of abstract concepts and the development of theorems for their own sake (Obeng-Denteh & Amoah-Mensah, 2011).

Nevertheless, it was clearly the case that each discipline selected in this study was associated with a particular set of epistemological paradigms and that these were inextricably linked to their writing practices, partly because it was via these practices that epistemological values were made manifest. Disciplinary writing practices were reified to a greater extent in some disciplines than others. The academics we spoke to who worked in marketing departments, for example, appeared less constrained by the expectations of peers and reviewers regarding disciplinary acceptance than those in history, for whom disciplinary identity was closely coupled to writing conventions.

In this chapter, we describe the specific genres and practices that our participants described as typical of, and valued within, their disciplines in relation to research writing, but also looking at pedagogical aspects of writing. In order to provide in-depth examples, we describe the different practices and values associated with writing historical monographs, marketing journal articles, and mathematical proofs. We look in particular at the extent to which such disciplinarily valued writing practices are seen to be under threat in the contemporary conditions of the higher education workplace, and at how our participants are defending and protecting the kinds of writing practices which constitute their discipline's processes of knowledge creation.

## Genres

Genre has been described as socially recognised ways of using language (Swales, 1990), and as a frame for social action (Bazerman, 1997; Miller, 1984). Bhatia (1993) and Swales (1990) have emphasised shared communicative purpose as the main criterion for categorising a set of texts within one genre. As we coded our data, we drew on these understandings to categorise the different genres that were mentioned by the academics we interviewed. In categorising these different genres, we took into account the interviewees' own social recognition of the texts they mentioned as representing a text type using language in a particular way towards a specific purpose.

The boundaries between one genre and another are not always clear-cut. Swales (1990), for example, argues that good news and bad news letters are different genres since they have different communicative goals, but Yates and Orlikowski (1992) argue that these would be sub-genres. The decision of how to distinguish a text type as a specific genre is ultimately an interpretive one.

It is also important to distinguish between genres and platforms. In this study, we did not categorise tweets, for example, as a genre, although all tweets share some discourse features in common, not least their tightly constrained length. One may tweet for many different communicative purposes, so we view tweets as one channel or platform of communication rather than a genre. Likewise, we considered emails and blogs to be mediums for communication, albeit with certain discourse features in common, rather than genres, although some discourse features characteristic of emails or of blog posts can be identified (Baron, 1998; Myers, 2010).

Despite the challenges in categorising genres, it is very clear from our data that academics need to write in many different genres for a very wide range of different purposes. The academics we interviewed mentioned around 100 different genres of writing. Many of these were the genres we expected: journal articles, teaching materials, and reports. Others were more surprising. Susan, for instance, a maths lecturer, when asked what kinds of writing she did, began by talking about emails and worksheets, and then told us she had started to write poetry, alone and with students, as a means of analysing qualitative data.

We categorised the genres we identified according to the type of work they related to: teaching, research, administration, or "service" (see Box 5.1). Later, in Chapter 8 where we discuss relationships and collaborations between people, we will see that some participants used the terms "admin" and "service" interchangeably. We categorised "service" as the sort of work that typically serves colleagues who may be in one's own or other institutions, or serves the broader discipline, and tends not to appear in departmental workload models. It includes genres such as writing reference letters, and reviews of books, journal articles, and grant applications. Research writing comprised the greatest number of different genres in our data, accounting for nearly 40% of genres mentioned. This was followed by administrative writing, at just over 30%, and service at just under 20%. Surprisingly, teaching-related writing accounted for only 13 different genres, or just over 10% of the total. Many of these genres were mentioned only once, however, and the number of times participants talked about the different genres may provide a better indication of their relative importance in academics' working lives.

---

**BOX 5.1 THE MULTIPLE GENRES OF ACADEMICS' WRITING**

Teaching-related writing included course outlines and validation documents, handouts, PowerPoint slides for lectures and many documents related to marking and giving student feedback.

Research-related writing included the complex paperwork for applying for research grants, including the proposals themselves and ethics statements; documenting and organising data collection; many kinds of research outputs from journal articles and books to popular summaries and press releases.

Administrative writing included writing agendas, inputting to databases, compiling job descriptions, reference letters, expenses claims, and explanations of policies and procedures (for example, quality assurance paperwork) for colleagues.

Service-related writing included evaluative reviews of articles and books, external examining reports, responding to surveys, and revising committee policies.

---

Our participants talked about research-related genres of writing most often, with over 40% of all mentions of genres of writing being about research, and the most frequently discussed single genre by far was the journal article. However, teaching-related genres were also frequently mentioned; the second most commonly talked about genre of writing overall was feedback to students, and the third was lecture slides.

In the context of universities, genres are often disciplinary constructs in that their purpose is recognised by the disciplinary community through shared discourse features such as structure, style, and content, as well as forms of repeated rhetorical conventions. This may include complex understandings of epistemology. In this sense, the concept of genre is useful as a form of boundary object (Star & Griesemer, 1989) because it serves a translatory function between two or more communities of practice. Genre is flexible enough to be adapted to disciplinary needs, yet robust enough to have a common identity recognisable across disciplines. Genres limit the meaning potential of a text and, in academia, realise disciplines by enacting accepted epistemological practices and rhetorical conventions. For example, what might be described as "core" academic genres such as research articles share certain properties in terms of style and structure as well as purpose, yet also vary across disciplines in their use of self-mention, evaluation, citation, and hedging language. These features of genres have been extensively studied (Hyland, 2015; Swales, 1990) and shown to index membership of a disciplinary group, while also demonstrating difference or individuality.

Genre is, therefore, closely linked to discipline and academic identity (Hyland, 2015; Ivanič, 1998; Lea & Stierer, 2011). Since disciplinarity and identity can be performed and inscribed over time through disciplinary writing (Hyland, 2015, p. 36), it is reasonable to hypothesise that practices around genre may be changing too. The three sections below describe the ways in which different forms of knowledge creation and genres of writing are valued and enacted in the disciplines of marketing, history, and mathematics.

## The knowledge that is valued in marketing

In this section, we describe the different practices and values associated with knowledge creation in the discipline of marketing. We look in particular at the pressures scholarly writing practices are under in contemporary marketing departments, and at how our participants respond to these pressures. We found genres dominated by journal articles, but still a concern for writing aimed at commercial interests, and some blurring of distinctions between professional practice writing and scholarly writing.

Marketing was one of the three disciplines in the study in which academics' writing practices were shaped most dramatically by the UK's Research Excellence Framework (REF) and institutional policies around it. For example, many marketing academics talked about their publications in terms of numerical values. This stems partly from the REF, which awards research outputs a star rating (with four-star being the best). For marketing academics, it also stemmed partly from their departments' use of target journal lists to guide their research writing towards high-ranking journals. The *ABS Journal Guide*, published annually by the Chartered Association of Business Schools, ranks academic journals in the field of business and management, including marketing, using a star rating system similar to that employed in the REF. Every marketing department participating in this study used this guide and encouraged their staff to publish in those journals it rated three- or four-star. This constrains marketing academics' publishing choices, particularly when it is linked to probation conditions (McCulloch, 2017), and it has been described as "fetishism" (Willmott, 2011) and "folly" (Tourish & Willmott, 2015).

Our participants tended to agree with these views. Michael, a professor of marketing, saw the use of journal rankings as "a very worrying development" because of its tendency to discourage risk-taking in research:

> the first three years [of an academic post] are coming now to become such a straightjacket in that the room for experimentation is limited ... this has been exacerbated in the UK by the publication of standard lists of journals ... and the way deans have tried to ... use that as some kind of tool to discipline, if you like, the probationers.

It is difficult to know where this pressure for a sanctioned list of target journals came from, given that the REF 2014 panel overview report for Panel C, into which the discipline of marketing falls, explicitly states that "grades awarded to outputs took no account of the journal in which the output was published" (REF, 2015a, p. 32). The same report also notes, however, that marketing as a discipline in the UK is both relatively small and somewhat threatened by a shortage of research-active staff to train and supervise doctoral candidates. It is likely that such evaluations influence the ways in which institutions and professional associations try to improve the REF performance of particular disciplines, and in turn, the guidance that they pass on to individual academics in those disciplines.

Another aspect of the REF that influenced marketing academics' writing practices was the notion of impact. This was important for marketing academics, many of whom had come into academia from professional careers and continued to work with user groups outside academia. This concern for societal impact is seen in this comment by Emma, who talks about the importance of her marketing research having real-world applications to commercial businesses as well as other academics: "I try and make sure that my research is actually actionable, and makes a difference to some business somewhere." Diane, a professor in marketing, also talked about what impact meant to her, describing it as a way of "changing the world":

> For me, impact is about my research and changing the world to people that will make use of my research in some way in their practical, everyday lives, so there isn't much of that because there's not time for it.

It is telling that Diane adds that she does not have enough time for impact-related writing. Genres such as white papers, articles for newspapers and online media, and articles in professional journals, all of which Diane had written as part of her academic role, were valued, but not prioritised and, instead, only engaged in if time allowed.

For the marketing academics we spoke to, writing for peer-reviewed academic journals was held in the highest esteem and brought the greatest rewards in terms of career advancement, to the extent that journal articles were described by Rose, the head of a marketing department, using the metaphor of currency: "Our currency is really journal articles." Other forms of scholarly publication such as monographs or book chapters were seen by marketing academics as far less important, with the former being mentioned just once by participants in this discipline, compared to journal articles, which were mentioned 21 times.

Pedagogically oriented genres of writing were also considered less prestigious than journal articles. Rose, who had written textbooks herself, talked about this in terms of value versus priority: "People who write textbooks: they are valued, because, obviously, they're really very good for the reputation of the department, and the students love it, but they're not seen as the priority activity."

These quotations illustrate the ways in which policies and institutions ascribe value to certain forms of knowledge creation over others, and show that the value of some genres of writing is more symbolic than actual. The ranking of marketing journals and inclusion of these rankings in publication targets means that marketing academics are pushed towards certain genres of writing and publication venues at the expense of others.

Although textbooks and non-academic genres were seen as being of secondary importance to scholarly research articles, there were occasions where one could be traded against the other. For example, in order to meet publication targets, which were often linked to conditions of probation, compromises were made between the high status of top-ranking journals and the work and time involved in getting papers accepted in such places. Publishing in trade magazines or publishing work based on consultancy rather than research was one way to achieve this. One lecturer in marketing, Emma, mentioned above, who was in her first academic post and still on probation, described her intention to submit a paper to the *Harvard Business Review*, a practice-oriented business magazine:

INTERVIEWER:  So it would help your probationary goals?
EMMA:  It would, yes, because I think people would read it. I think people will use it in teaching. Because the data is – on the negative side, because the study itself, it was a piece of consultancy work and some of the academic rigour was not as I would ideally have had it. I didn't do the data collection, somebody else did … I just thought it would be good to have a crack at the Harvard Business Review and see what happened. If you just have to write 1,000 or 700 words to get – I mean, if they say no straight

away, I've lost a day, and I can then turn that abstract into a paper for [a peer-reviewed journal].

Emma acknowledges that because the original work informing this article was consultancy rather than academic research per se, it was less rigorous than she might like. This is balanced, however, by the fact that such an article can be written relatively quickly and might be deemed as having "impact" through being widely read and taken up for practitioners' purposes.

These examples illustrate that drivers of decisions about which genres of writing academics should engage in come from several directions. One's own career goals and values, student expectations, reputational factors, and the REF all play a part, but the latter, perhaps because of its knock-on effect on so many other aspects of an institution and department's success, trumps all others. This is turn means that despite the wide range of genres academics want to and try to write, the peer-reviewed, three- or four-star journal article aimed primarily at other academics tends to dominate their efforts.

Genre can be used as a kind of classificatory tool in academia, and decisions on how writing is classified can be made on a pragmatic basis, leading to somewhat blurred distinctions between one genre and another. In the case of applied disciplines such as marketing, the boundaries between "scholarly" genres and "professional" ones such as consultancy reports were sometimes exploited for tactical reasons. For example, Diane described the challenges of getting ethics approval for research with commercial companies. She explains that in the world of business, "they meet you on Wednesday, they want you in on Thursday and they want to start the project on Friday". Diane's ethical clearance to conduct the research, however, took six months to obtain. She explained how she got round this problem of being stuck between two systems:

> I mean, if you treat it as consultancy, you don't need ethics. If you treat it as research, you need ethics approval, so I have treated it as consultancy to the point at which I've got clearance to do research and now it is research.

While being strategic in the ways work is classified can solve the problem of clashing expectations around timelines, blurring of genre boundaries can also have its downside. Diane went on to describe a context in which her transferral of genre norms from academic journal articles to consultancy work did not work out due to the differing expectations around confidentiality:

> I got stung with [a large company] where they said, "Yes, do this. Yes, do that", and then I wrote a paper and circulated it and they said, "You can't publish that". I said, "What do I do with it? It's about identity and branding and marketplaces; I can't obscure who you are", so now five years of work is basically unpublishable.

In this section, we have explored the academic writing practices of our participants in the discipline of marketing, and seen that institutional policies associated with the REF and, more broadly, the marketisation of higher education, including the use of performance targets and journal rankings, have a strong influence on the genres of writing that marketing academics focus their energies on. These findings lend further empirical support to the claims of scholars such as Gruber (2014), Mingers and Willmott (2012), Tourish and Willmot (2015), and Willmott (2011) that the use of journal guides has a deleterious effect on scholarship. We have also seen that academics may exploit the blurred boundaries between genres in order to operate successfully in this type of competitive environment. Marketing academics were, of course, not the only ones whose writing practices were affected by pressures associated with the REF. The next section reports on findings from our work with historians, which revealed that these pressures manifested themselves in this discipline in quite a different way.

## The knowledge that is valued in history

This section explores the practices and epistemic values associated with writing in the discipline of history. In particular, we found that the writing of historical monographs was seen as key to disciplinary prestige. For historians, creating knowledge often involved spending long hours in archives, accessing original sources, and spending years crafting a monograph. Historians tended to have a strong sense of what counted as knowledge and what counted as history, which could be constraining for those doing interdisciplinary work.

One clear finding to emerge from the study was that, in contrast to marketing academics, historians value the monograph rather than the journal article as their gold standard of publishing. Monographs were described by one of our participants, Rebecca, as, "the actual writing of the history". Monographs were understood to be sole-authored works, "usually the result of years of research in archives". The predominance of the monograph as a gold standard for publication in the discipline of history was also underlined by Harley, Acord, Earl-Novell, Lawrence, and Judson King in their US-based exploration of faculty values across seven disciplines (2010). The current study found, however, that the prestige of the monograph for historians was complicated by both practical and epistemic issues. In terms of the former, the main factor shaping their writing practices was time and pressures around the REF. Several historians used cooking metaphors to describe having a monograph "simmering" in the background, but being unable to proceed with it due to pressures to generate grant income or to publish other REF-able outputs. Natalie, for example, described being in a catch-22 situation of needing funding to complete the monograph she was planning (her next book), but feeling that she wouldn't be successful in getting funding until she had a monograph behind her.

It will be my next book but it continually has to go on the back burner. I've managed to give conference papers on it, I've managed to do bits of research on it but again I can't apply for the kind of grant that would give me the time to do that project in earnest until that first book is out.

For Natalie, the first monograph is the key that will open doors to funding, enabling her to take her research in the direction she wants. Bob also described his monograph as "bubbling under", and pointed to the pressure to produce material for the REF as barrier to making progress with it:

I've got a monograph bubbling under, which, I mean, in a way it's part of the advice that has been hanging over from the last REF, which was that, you know, monographs are great but you need four publishable outputs, you know.

Despite most historians' loyalty to the monograph, some were also coming to accept the importance of journal articles, partly driven by the demands of the REF. At the time this research was carried out, though the situation has changed since, to be "REF-able" meant to produce four research outputs in a four- to five-year period. Genre preferences were, therefore, complicated both by policy demands and by the notion of discipline. James, whose PhD was in history, but who now worked in a business school, said, "historians tend to think in terms of monographs rather than articles, but being in a business school I've sort of moved away from that somewhat".

As well as shaping their most valued genres of writing, discipline also influenced our participants' sense of identity. Academics in history tended to have a very clear understanding of what "being a historian" entailed for their writing. For example, Alex, a senior lecturer, said, "I also am wary, sometimes people say, 'Oh, I'm interdisciplinary.' Well, I don't think I am. I think I'm a historian". He explained that he did read work in other fields but described his writing as "Historical with a capital H". Asked what this meant, he said,

[it] boils down, essentially, in quite a practical way, you can point to the weight of the secondary sources with which you're engaging, the majority of which will be written by historians, circular though that may sound. And also to always having a framework of primary sources and a certain, I suppose, the primacy of having an archival base, so your contribution to knowledge will, in my research, always be based in some way in the sense that I'm bringing knowledge that I've analysed or that I've produced from the archives.

Thus, an important aspect of what it means to be a historian is to create knowledge based on archival material, from primary sources, in engagement with the work of other historians. Louis, who did more interdisciplinary work in the same department, talked about the challenges of getting historians to understand his work: "This causes a lot of problems because it means that often when my colleagues are reading it they say, 'This isn't history, this isn't history, this isn't history. I can't see the references to the primary research'."

Another participant, Dolly Blue, a professor who worked in an interdisciplinary area, pointed to a similar issue:

> The historians will always say, "Oh gosh, you didn't find this document yourself, how do you know about it?" I'll always say, "Well I'm trusting the historian. I'm not going to go and look at the bloody document, God almighty." I'd love to, but I don't have the time, the university doesn't have the money to get me to America. Working interdisciplinarily means that there are always people there ready to shoot you down.

The question of trust in other scholars and what this means to historians was closely linked to the sources and system of referencing they used in scholarly publications. Historians often write comprehensive footnotes, and they were used to this way of doing things, describing dreading being told to use an in-line referencing system. Verity explained:

> I'm a great sort of footnoter. I like doing them my way. I've yet to discover what my publishers actually require; I have a dread that it'll all be the Harvard system, in the text, and I like footnotes at the bottom of the page.

Louis described how the referencing system shaped the type of prior knowledge that could be invoked in a piece of writing. He explained that one reason for not including detailed references to primary sources in his writing for social science journals was due to the limitations of an in-line referencing system.

> When historians read it they just say, "This isn't research. These are just generalisations." You say, "Well, no. I have spelt out the research base on which this sits. I just haven't included it all." In an in-line Harvard style citation system you cannot do that.

Not all genres were equally unforgiving with regard to primary sources. Colin, another professor of history, was preparing a keynote speech for a symposium and described this as a genre where secondary research, albeit described in rather gruesome terms, was acceptable.

> I would look at some of them as original copies in our library or in a library in London. But I mean, this is the kind of thing where they're not expecting every sentence to be based upon original research. So I feel

quite happy to cannibalise other people's arguments or ideas with acknowledgement.

Overall, the extracts presented here from our interviews with historians reveal that, like the marketing academics, historians' scholarly writing was subject to pressures associated with the REF, but these took the form of pulling them away from their preferred genres in order to produce greater numbers of research outputs in a given period rather than pushing them towards meeting performance targets or demonstrating commercial impact. The historians in this study were particularly conscious not only of *what* they wrote, but also *how* they wrote it, in terms of what was signified by different discourse features. Specifically, they saw referencing systems and evidence of archival research as integral aspects of their discipline that acted as hallmarks of quality and disciplinary belonging. Academics in the third discipline we examined for this study, mathematics, also placed particular value on the material form and structure of their writing, as elegance and accuracy were seen as important features of good mathematics. It is this discipline to which we turn next.

## The knowledge that is valued in maths

In this third and final section of the chapter, we discuss the role that socio-material aspects of writing play in pedagogically oriented writing in the discipline of maths, as well as the kinds of genres, practices, and values that were associated with writing mathematical proofs.

Mathematics was an area in which the nature of the discipline had an important influence not only on scholarly writing for publications but also on writing for pedagogical purposes. Across all institutions in our data set, participants reporting doing marking electronically (see Chapter 8). However, because mathematics involves the use of formulae, which cannot easily be turned into electronic form without the use of LaTeX, practices in maths departments tended to be more flexible. Matt, the head of a school that included maths and computing, explained:

> There are areas where all the marking is done electronically ... There are places, if maths is a subject to talk about, there are places where it's viewed as not appropriate to get the students to produce an electronic piece of work. But that's not quite translating through into, or how we could use electronic assessment without necessarily having them to generate enormous amounts of word-processed mathematics, which is laborious.

Matt tacitly acknowledges that feedback practices are not always in step with what works in different disciplines. Maths was also something of an outlier in terms of the use of student handouts. While it is common practice these days for lecturers to upload teaching materials to a VLE, which students can then access online or print out materials from if they wish, Kirsty, an administrator in a maths department, noted that maths was the only department she knew of that routinely gave students hard-copy lecture notes, saying:

> Because it's mathematical, and I can see why. They produce notes with gaps, so students sit there in the lectures and they come to a point ... I don't know. I've not been to a lecture, but I think this is what happens. The lecturer goes through it, he gets to a point and he says, "Right, what answer do you think goes in here?" and they write it in. Sometimes, that's helpful, if it's a theorem or something. I think, with maths, it is quite different – that you have it written down in front of you

While many academics use PowerPoint to show slides when teaching, the mathematicians in our study expressed a strong preference for using traditional blackboards. In one of the universities we conducted the research in, classrooms dedicated to the teaching of mathematics had been designed in consultation with teaching staff, and had rows of blackboards across one wall. Robert, a professor of maths, explained why this was helpful:

> In maths you have to do all sorts of problems where, three boards on, you need to be able to refer to the way the argument went on. That process has to [be] up and visible. We still find that blackboards allow that visibility much better, I think, than most technological things.

He described having an argument on one blackboard, a statement of the theorem on another, and the development of the proof on the others, saying, "You can't expect people to remember how the argument went two boards ago now but they have to be able to look back." Thus, there was some resistance to the general move away from chalkboards, and the use of slides for teaching was not common among mathematicians.

This notion of the developing trajectory of an argument was also central to how mathematicians saw their own processes of knowledge creation in their scholarly writing, and this could also involve the aid of a blackboard. Will explained:

> It is a process where a lot of the actual producing mathematics is standing at a board, talking with somebody, writing on paper, just sketching things on paper until you see that you have actually got a result, something that you can prove. Then at that point you might try and type it up to force yourself to check the details.

Several mathematicians described similar ways of doing maths, as a low-tech process involving scrap paper or a board, and characterised by setbacks. Will continued:

This might be at a board. You are trying to come up with something. You can be stuck for a long time just getting nowhere but then you get an idea; you try to sketch it out on paper to see if the details seem to be working out. Then at that point you will try to either write or type it up carefully. That forces you to actually check details and to really follow the logic of the arguments more carefully.

This knowledge production process is very similar to that described by one of Kuteeva and McGrath's informants, in that the writing represents an attempt to prove something the researcher believes to be true, and could thus be described as "knowledge verification" (Kuteeva & McGrath, 2015, p. 232).

In terms of preferred genres, the journal article was seen by the mathematicians in this study as the default research output. They seldom mentioned monographs and did not mention edited collections at all. In common with the genres favoured by marketing academics, the journal article was the dominant genre of research writing for mathematicians, but this was not perceived as having significantly changed, therefore pressure to produce journal articles was not described as a threat to the disciplinary identity of mathematicians. Similarly, none of the participants working in mathematics described being asked to target their writing at any particular journals.

Although the mathematicians in the study produced many of the same genres as participants in other disciplines, the process of writing these differed. Whereas historian Rebecca had described preparing monographs as "writing the history", for many of the mathematicians, writing was a separate process from that of doing the mathematics, which tended to precede "writing up".

WILL: When I say, "doing the mathematics", I mean doing the work that we are then later writing up into a paper.
INTERVIEWER: You made a difference between the maths and the writing.
WILL: That's right, there is, yes. The maths is – the pure maths is I mean, you are trying to prove results. That means there is some statement you think might be true – I mean, you may later change your mind – but you are trying to come up with an argument for why it is true. In the end, it has to be a very precise argument, one that would be accepted by other mathematicians.

Will's comment also reveals that disciplinary acceptance for mathematicians may lie less in methodological concerns and referencing norms, as it did for historians, and more in the qualities of the proof, such as precision of argument. Other aspects of writing maths that were valued included aesthetic concerns, as Robert's comment shows:

What you can do is you can say, after I've done quite a complicated bit of analysis, have I done anything stupid? Okay, it's either right or it's wrong. Assuming I haven't done anything stupid, it's right. Then there's a question – let me show you – then there's a question of partly do I believe it, partly does it look pretty.

The writing of maths has an important justificatory function, in that it must convince the reader that the proof is correct, but it should also be elegant. This is in keeping with findings by McGrath and Kuteeva (2012) that the aesthetic qualities of a proof boosted the perceived importance of findings. In contrast, the usefulness of research was, for pure mathematicians at least, not an important marker of value:

INTERVIEWER:   What about is it doable? Is it practicable? Does that come
                        into it?
ROBERT::   Well no, because I don't care about that.

In this sense, impact of the sort that concerned the marketing academics in this study was of less interest to those in the discipline of mathematics, although this may have been a particularly strong tendency for those at the pure end of the maths continuum. Ian, when asked if he used social media to disseminate findings, replied that he did not and added, "I mean, for mathematicians, hardly anybody can understand what our research is about".

   In general, the mathematicians in this study talked less than those in other disciplines about the pressures being exerted on their writing by forces such as research evaluation regimes and pressures to demonstrate impact, despite that fact that the REF 2014 panel overview report (2015b, p. 41) notes that the boundaries of the unit of assessment into which mathematics were subject to change given the degree of interdisciplinary cross-referrals. Mathematicians in this study tended not to see writing as the primary means of thinking about maths, but rather as a means of refining and justifying the argument. The process of doing maths was one of gradually testing out all the steps of argumentation of a complex proof and eventually producing something that was both "right" and "pretty". The most valued genre of scholarly writing was the journal article, and this had been little influenced by wider changes in higher education. In this sense, the mathematicians in this study appeared to enjoy a greater sense of epistemological security than those in both marketing and history.

## Conclusions

In summary, genre continues to be an important tool for understanding and enacting disciplinarity and academic identity, albeit a site of some contention. In all three disciplines examined here, the peer-reviewed academic journal article was a key means of producing and disseminating knowledge, but while this was relatively unproblematic for mathematicians, it was a source of tension in marketing and history because institutional policies around the REF were driving changes in the forms of knowledge being privileged, which conflicted with disciplinary traditions (Tight, 2000). Elsewhere, we have talked about the REF as having introduced a dominant "genre regime" in universities (Tusting, 2018) which privileges and rewards publication in some genres and locations over others. In particular, in the case of marketing, the findings discussed in this chapter demonstrate the role of contextual factors such as institutional policies and discipline-specific journal rankings in acting as systems for managing academics' writing and publishing practices (Shepherd, 2018). This exploration of discipline and genre in academics' writing practices has highlighted the situated nature of academic literacy (Barton & Hamilton, 2000; Paltridge et al., 2016; Tusting, 2012) through the ways in which our participants value different forms of knowledge creation. This is refracted through their personal biographies and career goals, as well as institutional and departmental practices, national policies, and disciplinary norms. It is clear that the demands of the REF play out differently across different disciplines, and often conflict with long-held disciplinary values.

# 6

# CHANGING TOOLS AND TECHNOLOGIES IN ACADEMICS' WRITING LIVES

## Introduction and background

So far we have examined the broad influences on contemporary change in academics' working lives, such as managerialism and growing marketisation. We have identified disciplinary differences and how new genres of writing are developing. In this chapter we take a closer look at tools and technologies which are leading to changes in academics' writing and what it means to be an academic. This includes tools and platforms provided by universities, such as virtual learning environments (VLEs) and online library resources, as well as social media, smartphones, and portable devices which academics may bring into the workplace from their everyday lives. Their deployment can lead to new practices and every aspect of academic work can be seen to be changing as a result of them.

Drawing on our data we show the wide range of digital tools and platforms used in writing. As well as some disciplinary differences, there are individual differences in academics' take up and reliance on particular practices. In the interviews it was very clear that people had strong likes and dislikes and they were happy to express feelings towards particular software and platforms. Analysing people's stances proved revealing in terms of the reception and use of new tools and technologies. In this chapter we outline our approach to affect and stance-taking and use it to trace the individual paths people take in tool usage in their professional lives.

There are different paths to common goals, and the ways academics use tools and technologies in their professional lives connects to the kind of scholar they see themselves to be, and more broadly to their understanding of academic work. As we have already seen in Chapter 4, new digital technologies can lead to an "always on" experience of work. On the one hand, this can enable emancipatory possibilities: flexible working, easy access to intellectual resources, reaching new and wider audiences. But alongside this, some critics have warned of a more "accelerated academy" through academics' relationship with digital technologies combined with increased workloads, leading to stress, anxiety, and a feeling of time pressure limiting scope for reflexivity (Carrigan, 2015b). Academics are often left to work out and navigate the landscape of new technologies themselves, and therefore end up holding a number of stances on its use in different aspects of their professional life.

The current chapter explores some of these different stances. This is through the discovery of forms of *positive affect* in relation to, for example, how various forms of collaboration are enhanced by digital tools. Contrasted with this there is considerable *negative affect* expressed, particularly in relation to how new technologies are invasive and people feel the pressure to be "always on" and available to others. These issues are explored through two case studies: how people utilise PowerPoint in very different ways in structuring their academic writing; and how email is seen as both a blessing and a curse. This chapter emphasises how technologies need to be discussed in the context of other contemporary social changes and that the stresses and frustrations of being "always on" reflect broader social concerns about people's control over the mediatisation of all aspects of everyday life.

## Digital tools and resources

In the past two decades there has been a transformation in the tools and resources available in the academic workplace. As we saw in the vignettes in Chapter 3, and in the discussions of space and time in Chapter 4, academics have access to a wide range of digital tools and resources which they use in their work in diverse ways. File-sharing and other tools provide new affordances for collaborative work. Video-conferencing enables face-to-face contact with colleagues and students over great distances. Online university systems make administrative processes directly accessible from any computer, from claiming expenses and booking rooms through to managing student attendance and making research publications open access. Online library resources have become the main way in which people access journal articles and, increasingly, ebooks. Libraries are exploring new roles as stakeholders in knowledge production rather than as repositories of physical volumes, for example in putting on graduate courses in research methods and information management. In our data, we identified 60 different digital platforms academics were using.

Universities now provide VLEs, mentioned in earlier chapters, which bring together academics, students, and administrators, facilitating distance and blended learning and collaboration. These VLEs are spaces in which many different digital tools and technologies are integrated for purposes related to teaching and learning. These include slides from presentation software, lecture capture, forum discussions, online assessment submission, grading tools, and plagiarism detection software, among others. They serve curricular as well as administration purposes. The substantial investment they require can follow cumbersome procurement and consultation procedures involving workplace activities such as forum meetings with staff and students, and competitive tender with suppliers. This investment is usually so high-stakes that it brings with it an institution-wide regime of professional development and training to ensure all the academics within a university are up to speed on how to use a new VLE.

VLEs now shape how academics interact with students. They can lead to new forms of collaboration with university administrative staff, as well as with computing staff and librarians. Nevertheless, they are often adopted with little or no appreciation of how they will impact the writing work of academics. Utilising a VLE is often mandatory in institutions and this draws attention to issues of compulsion which we return to later in this chapter. In terms of writing, the dominance of VLEs raises questions about ownership of: the written content; reuse of teaching materials; open resources; and the time and investment needed for familiarisation and training.

Most of the tools discussed so far are those provided by the institution. Another development is the way in which everyday devices are brought into the workplace. Smartphones and portable devices like iPads which may have been bought for use in everyday life then get used in academic life. There has been a shift in this even during the two years of data collection for the project, as platforms like Dropbox, WhatsApp, Facebook, and Skype have shifted from the everyday sphere into the workplace. Devices may be owned by the university, for example where they are given to researchers on projects; more often, they are owned personally and used for work purposes.

The notion of boundaries and boundary crossing was discussed in Chapter 4. The use of everyday digital tools and artefacts in the workplace is another way in which literacy practices cross over boundaries between different contexts. In the Literacy for Learning in Further Education project (see Ivanič et al., 2009) boundary crossings provided evidence that college learners who are deemed to have low levels of literacy can be sophisticated users of texts and technologies outside of their college (e.g. at home or at work). Similarly, Bhatt (2017a) advances the concept of "irruption" to describe how successful student writing necessitated the mobilisation of digital literacy practices which originated from somewhere other than the classroom (for example from friendship groups, families, work documents, etc.). Digital media use, therefore, resulted in literacy practices from unforeseeable places as part of institutional writing; a phenomenon we can also see when academic writers draw on their everyday practices and bring them into the workplace context.

## Digital communications technologies and academics' writing practices

Turning to how digital communications technologies are shaping academics' writing practices, let us go to the people we interviewed and what they talked about, to build up a picture of what is going on in terms of academics writing. This data came largely from their techno-biographic interviews. So, how are they using the wealth of available tools and platforms?

We start with four brief examples of specific people who reported drawing upon a wide range of digital tools and platforms in their writing. Diane, a social scientist from the marketing department of her university, wrote in Word. She often used Skype for meetings and took screenshots of documents in her research activities. She used shared Dropbox folders for version control when writing papers. Gareth, a mathematician mentioned earlier, wrote using Word along with LaTeX, a maths text editor, sending documents back and forth using LaTeX which his student compiled. He used email, but hardly used the university's VLE.

Rebecca, a historian, reported that digital cameras had revolutionised collection of archive material; nevertheless she still liked to hand-write manuscripts. Don, another historian, reported limited use of digital tools in research, mainly confining himself to Word. In addition, he reported innovative collaborative teaching using the VLE. This was driven by requests from faculty. With his research, he still took pencil notes on index cards in records offices. Handwriting was restricted to fewer practices. The departmental stationery cupboard had left-over index cards, glue sticks, Tipp-Ex, treasury tags, and other items which are no longer used. Note how people have considerable control and have their own particular configurations of devices and platforms used in writing.

Just as in the earlier study we carried out in 2009 referred to in Chapter 1 (Satchwell et al., 2013), the people we interviewed mentioned the role of technologies extensively, often expressing strong liking or hating of various platforms and devices with strong expressions of stance and of affect. A theme which is a shift from 2009 is that in 2016 there was more compulsion: using the university's VLE was effectively optional in 2009 but was now largely compulsory in the institutions we researched as a way of communicating with students. Marking and feedback have to be done online; the library will often only get the online version of a book. We traced how these changes then led to new practices, for example with more overview of marking and providing feedback to students. This used to be a personal communication between teacher and student, whereas now course leaders and administrative staff also have access to it.

There have always been some things one can do at home. In earlier times in some departments people were almost expected not to come into office on Fridays, but to stay at home and "do research". Academic work has always been mobile and restless. Nevertheless, in the past you could go home from this peripatetic life and not be followed by administration, and other emails. It was the digital tools which enabled the freedom from the office. From the examples earlier, we can see that this non-digital issue, that of office space, very quickly turns into an issue of digital mediatisation. Technology enables escaping from the office, and working at home, working on emails, marking, and writing in different places. Work ceases to be a place, it becomes an activity, a practice which can "take place" anywhere.

## What annoys you about technology at work? Affect and stance-taking

One question in our interviews turned out to be quite revealing: what annoys you about technology at work? Academics were keen to answer this question, often at length, and were very passionate about their likes and hates. Their answers covered many topics: loving or hating Twitter; being annoyed if people are on their phones or iPads in classes; loving their smartphone and how they can look up the meaning of words in the middle of other people's talks, or Google people to see what they have published; and having iPhone anxiety if they cannot feel it in their pocket or see it close by.

In fact, this liking and hating was a good way to engage people in the topic and has proved very helpful when examining changes in people's writing practices. We will refer to this expression of affect as "stance-taking". The concept of stance-taking is useful in sociolinguistics and discourse analysis. It brings together a wide range of work on people's attitudes and how they position themselves in relation to what they are referring to in different contexts. Stance is broadly defined as the positioning and evaluation people make of what they or others are expressing at any time. Jaffe (2009, p. 3) defines stance-taking as "taking up a position with respect to the form or the content of one's utterance". The stance expressed may refer to the stance-taker, to others, or to the content of the utterance. Bringing together existing work on stance, there are two main kinds of stance: epistemic stance, which is basically claims of knowledge, belief, authority, etc. towards stance objects, for example "I think ...", "I believe ...", and affective stance – the stance-taker's feelings (often evaluative) towards a stance object, for example, "I like ...". This may be signalled by explicit discourse markers such as "I believe" or "I like", but much of the time stances are implicit and are inferred from the utterance and its surrounding context even without these overt markers. Of course, affective stance is common in social networking where users are constantly invited to evaluate and to say what they like or don't like. For more on stance-taking in social media, see Barton and Lee (2013).

We examined affective stance as it was expressed in the interviews. It was identified first by reading the transcripts and coding them for affect, and second by searching the whole data set for examples of affect terms such as "like", "love", "enjoy". For instance, Verity, a historian, expressed strong positive affect for her job. Spread over a one-hour interview, she made the following comments:

> I do actually like teaching ... I love the third year course I do ... it's just great fun to teach ... I quite like lecturing. I mean, I like doing workshops, I like doing seminars, but I quite enjoy lecturing and it's quite nice ... and it's lovely using PowerPoint ... Research, I really like doing research; it's lovely doing archival research ... I actually quite like writing; I find it demanding, but sort of quite exciting.

We can see here how a positive affective stance towards the technology of PowerPoint is making a contribution to her overall positive evaluation of her lecturing experience. But, as we will see, positive expressions of affect were not the only ones present in our data. We also searched for terms such as "dislike" and "hate". At one point Charles, who has been discussed earlier, stated, "I hate Skype ... I find Skype debilitating ... I find it's a simplistic thing, the dislocation between eye contact". He preferred meeting face-to-face, spending the day with people, having coffee breaks and dividing work tasks. There are many more such examples of negative affect towards technologies in our data.

Concentrating on expressions of affect enabled us to explore our central question of how digital communications technologies are shaping academics' writing practices. First we will explore the range of stance expressed and individual variation. Often, as in the examples above, affect was expressed towards devices and platforms, such as iPhones, Skype, Twitter, or PowerPoint. Each person seemed to have a personal profile of stances towards the range of devices and platforms they utilised. To continue with Charles, he wrote using Word and used Dropbox to synchronise documents between his computers. He linked this to his physical office: "for each pile there that represents a project that we're working on, but like anything most of it's actually in Dropbox, which alarms me but it's easy", showing a mixed affective stance towards Dropbox, appreciating its convenience while not completely trusting it. He also used the qualitative software NVivo to code data, and described this in positive terms as "a real hands-on analysis". By focusing on affect it is possible to see more clearly some of the reasons for the individual differences shown in people's uses of tools and platforms.

### Different paths to common goals: PowerPoint as a form of writing

Such differences can be seen when people take individual routes to common ends, such as arranging a meeting, or providing student feedback on an assignment. Preparing presentations is one example of a writing goal which can be achieved in a range of ways, using different technologies. Don, a historian mentioned earlier, explained how he wrote papers from scratch in Word, how conference papers were written-to-be-read, and how he used PowerPoint images to illustrate his paper as he spoke. However, other people reported different practices around using PowerPoint, for instance by placing the main structure of their argument on the slides in bullet point form.

People used it in different ways for different purposes, especially distinguishing presenting conference papers from giving lectures to students. When presenting, most people used some sort of notes as a support. These could be the actual words on the PowerPoints or they could be separate notes. Several people had a script of some sort which they read or had partly memorised. This was especially true for conference papers. Don prepared a complete written paper for any conference presentation. PowerPoints, he said, were "for images, not text". Verity said the same. Don would have roughly 12 slides for a 40-minute paper. He saw himself as "not particularly good at talking from slides". Like others, he would go through the paper several times before the actual presentation to get more fluent at the reading and wanted "to make it sound as if it wasn't being read". A few people actually memorised the whole script, effectively turning it into a performance.

Teaching was usually approached differently. Don, for instance, would "ad lib more" and wanted to give the impression of a lecture not being a written text. PowerPoints for teaching would be revised incrementally year on year. Several people said that their practices had changed over time as they gained experience in teaching, moving away from reading a script to having less reliance on it. Rebecca, also a historian, explained how her foundation point for a lecture used to be a fully written out script, but now PowerPoint slides with images formed her starting point and the text was in her head. This was partly so that she could keep control over the content that she had produced from researching, teaching, and writing over the years. PowerPoint seems to provide people with a range of possibilities for individual routes for the creation of texts for presentation and sometimes eventually for publication.

There are, of course, alternatives to PowerPoint. People had strong reactions to some other presentation software, such as Prezi, views on which ranged from "I prefer Prezi" to "Prezi makes me vomit". However, in our data in general, people did not tend to express strongly affective stance towards PowerPoint either positively or negatively. Instead, they usually talked of it in quite neutral terms, seeing it as the default software for a lecture or conference paper.

## Conflicted stance: email, a blessing or a curse?

In contrast to the neutral stance often displayed towards PowerPoint, email was associated with a much more negative affective evaluation. The interviews generated 295 pages of data about emails. About 2% of these quotations were about the positive affordances of email (discussing in what ways it was helpful or useful); the rest of them were critical in some way. Email is viewed almost entirely negatively by our participants. This emotional and practical salience of email (and its difficulties) for all of our participants was an unexpected finding.

Academics' everyday professional writing practices are very extensively mediated through email. It was by far the most commonly mentioned digital platform for writing across our 75 interviewees. As one of them told us, "Everything is done by email now." It is the default means of communication. Email is omnipresent. People have it on every device. They mentioned it in passing when discussing other topics, and they were keen to talk more about it. People mentioned a wide range of writing activities in relation to email, including: preparing grant applications, journal articles and job references; organising events, arranging meetings; emailing tweets for someone else to tweet; emailing reminders to oneself; keeping a record of interactions; and ordering equipment.

Given this ubiquity of email in the ecology of academics' communication, and particularly given that email has been a feature of the academy for more than 30 years, we might assume that established expectations and patterns around working with emails would have developed by now. However, our research reveals an enormous diversity in practices and attitudes. The common theme is that everyone seems to be struggling to keep up with email; they are trying to do this in many different ways.

Our participants used a range of different devices for checking or writing emails. Many used their personal mobile phones. Several said that tablets were quicker to "fire up" than laptops, so they would check emails on an iPad or other tablets at home. This sometimes meant that people had to do what Jarrahi, Nelson, and Thomson (2017) call "configuration work" and part of what Lambert (2016) refers to as "shadow work": setting up particular combinations of devices and platforms for different tasks and trying to make them communicate smoothly with each other. This includes, for example, trying to get Apple devices to work with Windows, setting up virtual private networks to access university services, and so on.

Unsurprisingly, the mobility of these devices meant that when we asked people where and when they tended to deal with emails, the answer was "everywhere". The huge majority checked email at home as well as at work, and usually not just within working hours. The experience of getting up at 5.30 or 6 am to check email before going to work was very common. One of our participants called this a "pre-check" and then she came to work and responded to more from there.

Most people expressed a sense of a loss of control around email, as Colin described:

> And working either at home or at work I access email and that can be a blessing but also a curse, because I'm not very self-disciplined as I think some people are to say, "Emails I shall attend to between 6:00pm and 7:00pm or 4:00pm and 5:00pm". I've never got into that habit. The email

beeps or something pops up and I open it ... you never know if something's very urgent or not.

Positive stance and negative stance can be identified, but sometimes both are expressed at the same time, as in Colin's phrase here "a blessing but also a curse". He was not alone in taking this position. Others were similarly conflicted in expressing what they thought of email. It enabled them to be mobile and deal with work anywhere, while at the same time it followed them everywhere and they could not get away from it. We refer to this as *conflicted stance*. To some extent expressing contrary views is a way of dealing with change. It is also a way of coping. Email can be good but too much of it is stressful, and overload of email was one of the key issues people identified.

The ways academics talked about their email, the language and specifically the metaphors they used, show more about their attitudes towards it. Metaphor is a way of understanding one domain in terms of another; in Lakoff and Johnson's (1980) terms, understanding the target domain in terms of the source domain. In the case of the data we present here, email is the target domain (the one that needs a more concrete domain to describe it), and our participants drew on a range of source domains to represent email metaphorically. Some of them went as far as to evoke the domain of horror: "email is of course this spectre that looms over modern academic life". We identified all the different metaphorical expressions people used about email and grouped them to identify patterns which help us to understand people's experiences.

The first type of metaphor is to do with email as associated with heaviness or large volume. Some of these drew on metaphors of bursting or overflowing, evoking a sense of overload, as in Louis' description of a cascade: "Unless it is something that is going to require a lot of work I try and do it there and then because otherwise I find they get lost in the cascade, the infinite email cascade", or Fiona's vision of her inbox, combining the metaphors of too much liquid with the notion of bursting: "My inbox, which is already always overflowing, would completely explode if I sent misleading, unclear emails." These are metaphors which connote capacity being exceeded. While it is technically possible for an email inbox to be full, the consequence would not be an explosion or an overflow but merely emails bouncing back to the sender until the situation is resolved. Here, by using these metaphors, Louis and Fiona are signalling their personal feelings of overwhelm by email, a very common theme in our data.

Developing on from the idea of load, the second common grouping was email represented as an ongoing bombardment, drawing on metaphors of battle or self-defence, of continually fighting off the emails. These metaphors convey the idea of emails as a constant inflow of danger from which people need to constantly protect themselves; as Josh said, "a lot of my days are sometimes just fending off emails". Another common way of talking about email was as an entity with its own behaviour which people try to train or to keep control of but don't always manage to. Stephanie, a head of department, said that "control of my inbox is almost like a symbolic proxy for control of my whole work life". This example is slightly different from the examples of overflow and bombardment, in that the academic at least has a more active role in trying to keep control.

A related group of metaphors came from the domain of housework, talking about dealing with emails in terms of cleaning or clearing out rubbish or clutter. In Chapter 3, we saw how both Ian and Gareth talked about clearing out or cleaning out emails regularly. Gareth said, "I used to be able to get on with very substantial things, whereas now, 50% of it is constantly looking back at email and clearing out emails".

These metaphors can be better understood if we examine the specific issues that people identify around email. Reinforcing the notion that stances adopted towards email were predominantly negative, of the 707 data quotes on email, 135 quotations identified a specific problem with email. We grouped these into seven different types of problem. People get *too many* emails; no matter how many they received in a day, from 20 to 200, people felt their incoming load was too great. There was *too much variety* in the emails, and this came in unpredictably. Any given email might require a one-word answer, or it could be attached to several long attachments requiring reading and action. Email is *hard to escape*, being present on phones and tablets, at home and at work; and email is felt to *take away time and autonomy*, with the demands of email encroaching on other important tasks. Emails can be *hard to write*, getting the level of formality and tone appropriate is difficult, particularly for emails about tricky personal or professional issues. They can be *hard to understand*, and misunderstandings can lead to problems with students or colleagues. Finally, email is felt to be habitually *used for the wrong purposes*, for long group discussions or difficult decisions where face-to-face communication would be more efficient or effective.

Such tensions around email use are not, of course, unique to academia. In Chapter 4, we discussed O'Carroll's (2008) research with IT professionals, and their lack of a clear distinction between "working" time and "not working" time. The constant monitoring of email – checking and responding – exacerbated this experience. For O'Carroll's research participants, in a social workplace where communication was very important, email represented both an important work task to keep on top of, and a potential interruption fragmenting the day.

> Email is ... ambiguous. Each one might take a couple of seconds to read, but dealing with all of them might take a morning or an afternoon. It is short and fragmented, yet also time consuming. It is neither all work, nor all non-work.
>
> *(O'Carroll, 2008, p. 185)*

This ambiguity of experience and the multiple problems associated with managing email make it a challenge for people to develop strategies for managing email that are effective. People tried using a range of strategies. They categorised emails, dealing with important ones first, quick ones first, or ones from students first, or deliberately leaving long and difficult ones until later. They deliberately responded as quickly as possible, or aimed to keep their inbox below a certain number, or to empty it once a day – the "inbox zero" strategy. A few set clear boundaries around email time, dealing with it once a day. Some took great care over drafting emails to make them clear and setting clear subject lines, to avoid confusion.

Unfortunately, none of these strategies solved all of the problems participants identified. The categorising strategy addresses the problem of the variety of emails, but not the problem of volume. Responding quickly or focusing on inbox zero addresses the problem of volume, but perpetuates the ever-present hard-to-escape nature of email. Setting boundaries around email time protects other tasks from the intrusion of email, but does not minimise the volume that needs to be dealt with. Taking time for clarity addresses miscommunications but adds to the problem of limited time.

The data show that the problems that email presents cannot be easily solved by the strategies people are trying, and they have tried many things. Linking up with the metaphors, "load" and "bombardment" convey the most central problems people are facing. "Cleaning", "clearing" and "controlling" convey the strategies that they are adopting. However, there is a disjuncture between metaphors of constant danger coming at you, and metaphors of systematic organisation: you cannot keep "fending off" a "constant bombardment" forever, and you cannot stop an "infinite cascade" by "clearing it up". In these ways, the metaphors used provide insight into the real double-binds of the experience of emails in academic working lives.

The metaphor of overload is a powerful one and has been used before. The particular idea of "email overload" dates back more than two decades to a study by Whittaker and Sidner (1996) who studied office workers' emails. Their results were not unlike the data we have collected 20 years on. People emphasised the advantages of being able to communicate with colleagues across space and time, but they also expressed concerns about being overwhelmed by the task of keeping up-to-date with their emails. Like our study, they also found that people had very different strategies for managing emails, ranging from users who kept all their emails in their inbox through to those who filed everything away in folders each day as soon as possible and kept their inboxes clear.

Replications of their work and other similar studies since then (such as Bellotti, Ducheneaut, Howard, Smith, & Grinter, 2005; Fisher, Brush, Gleave, & Smith, 2006; Karr-Wisniewski & Lu, 2010; Grevet, Choi, Kumar, & Gilbert, 2014) have told the same story: that while the number of emails received has gone up, but not by an enormous amount, people's concerns about emails and the stress they describe has increased consistently.

Whittaker and Sidner (1996) make an important point about email overload, using the phrase in a different way. They suggest that the email software is itself being overloaded: email is being used for purposes it was not designed for. Email was designed as a non-synchronous communication platform – simply, for sending messages. Increasingly, in the academic sphere and elsewhere, email is being used as a task management system, delivering complex tasks as attachments and links, and as a message filing system, archiving records of communication in increasingly complex folder systems. Innovations such as flagging, linking conversations, and ever-more powerful search functions have been added to many email platforms to facilitate these uses.

Some of our videography data shows academics using these features in sophisticated ways. For instance, Don was recorded while writing a pre-viva report in preparation for a PhD examination. He kept his email interface open during the session, in order first to locate the pro forma he needed to fill in, and then to check back on previous correspondence about the examination. However, because the email interface was open, he also checked for new emails which had come in while working on the report, and regular email notification sounds accompanied his writing. One of the incoming emails was another PhD examining request, asking for information about his previous examining roles. He quickly located these details in correspondence relating to an earlier viva in his email folders, adjusted it to add his the current examining role, and sent it straight back. We see here how email enables the co-ordination of working activities at high speed, facilitated by the storing and searching functions of the archive (indeed, our videography data overall showed academics spending more time searching for information electronically than they displayed conscious awareness of in the interviews). At the same time, we see how using email in this way opens Don up to the kinds of interruptions associated with the constant inflow discussed above. This raises the question of whether email is fit for the purposes which academics and other workers are using it for.

The issues we identify here around email are, of course, symptoms of the larger issues discussed already around acceleration and intensified management of academic work. Email is a conduit of these processes, whereby academics feel they are getting ever-busier, having more demands placed upon them, and carrying out a wider variety of writing tasks. As a result, everything feels speeded up, they have less control over their lives, and boundaries between work and non-work are collapsing. The tendency amongst our participants is to individualise these experiences. For instance, Pippa, a professor of marketing, told us, "I'm really rubbish with email". We would argue that on the basis of this data, Pippa should not be placing the blame for her issues with email within her lack of email efficiency; her difficulties, like those of others in our data, are evidence of wider systemic issues.

In this chapter, we have seen the variety of different technologies academics are now using in their writing. We have examined the issues that this can raise and have explored how they talk about and adopt stances towards these technologies. This provides insights into broader issues of academic working life. One of the large changes in relation to communications technologies in the past 15 years or so has been the rise of social media, which has opened up a range of new possibilities for academic writing, but also poses many challenges. The next chapter will focus in on this issue.

# 7

# NEW SOCIAL MEDIA GENRES

## Marketing the academic self

### Introduction: new social media genres in academia

The contemporary academic workplace requires people to engage in new forms of writing which produce not only representations of knowledge, but also public representations of themselves. This chapter focuses on academics writing on social media, conceived broadly as referring to all online platforms where participants can make writing public without the gatekeeping of an institutional publisher. With the post-REF 2014 "impact agenda" (Watermeyer, 2016), social media has become one site where academics feel under increased pressure to engage in new genres of writing, on new platforms, for new audiences. Impact and public engagement can be interpreted in different ways, but for many, it involves the social and public aspects of Weller's (2011) notion of "digital scholarship": disseminating research and sharing ideas online via blogs, tweets, and academic networking sites. In this chapter we explore the pressures academics experience to engage in this sphere, and the diversity of their responses to such pressures.

We do not discuss in this chapter the impact of institutional repositories in which academics are increasingly compelled to deposit selected information for REF purposes and for universities to display on their own websites. Neither do we deal extensively with Google Scholar, which similarly presents a public profile regardless of the individual academic's engagement with it. Individuals may not like the way they find themselves represented on such sites, but they have little say over this, in contrast to interactive social media where they can choose how and how much to engage.

This is an area where expectations have changed rapidly over the last decade or so. While online spaces such as blogs and virtual communities have existed since the 1990s, they remained largely the province of enthusiasts until software and platforms emerged in the mid-2000s to make online writing easy to upload for the general population – spoken of as the advent of Web 2.0 communication. Merchant (2009) discusses the characteristics of Web 2.0: coined by O'Reilly (2005), the term indicates an interactive and collaborative space in which users actively create and design an online presence and participate in a community of like-minded users generating content together. While academics were quick to adopt the possibilities associated with email communication (along with all its challenges, as discussed in the previous chapter), writing on Web 2.0 and social media was less rapidly integrated into the academic world. For some time there was suspicion of those who engaged with social media. It was seen to take time that could more usefully be used for writing in traditional academic genres – journal articles, chapters, and monographs. However, as we shall see later, institutional encouragement to engage with social media was becoming more common. As Ian, a mathematician, told us,

> My perception used to be that social media was considered a bit time wasting or frivolous, whereas now it seems to have gone almost the other way, where if you're not doing it, something is wrong. It's become this bit of unspoken pressure, perhaps, or self-imposed pressure. You see other people doing it and wonder, should I be doing that as well?

## Practices on different social media platforms

The range of different social media platforms which provide academics with opportunities for public writing online is huge. As one might expect, Facebook and Twitter were mentioned most frequently in our data, but other platforms included personal and institutional blogs, academic networking sites, disciplinary discussion forums, online business networking sites, and others. Many of the genres associated with these online platforms (the tweet, the blog post, the personal webpage) address different publics from the traditional academic genres of the journal article and monograph, are networked in new ways, and operate on very different timescales. Many of these genres of online self-representation entail elements of self-promotion, in addition to enabling public representations of knowledge work. While such genres have some continuities with the kind of promotional work that has always gone on through traditional media like newspapers and TV interviews, the academics we spoke to regarded them differently and felt that they required new skills.

Where people were using social media, they often used different sites for different purposes, with a key distinction being made between personal and professional use (another kind of boundary to add to those discussed in Chapter 4). James was planning to start a personal blog, but not a professional one. For several people, Facebook was used for more personal purposes and Twitter for more professional ones. Diane used Twitter exclusively for professional reasons. Verity's initial attempted engagements with Facebook and Twitter ended rapidly when she realised the potential for blurring between her professional and personal lives: "I tried to do Facebook some years ago, and all these students wanted to be my friend on Facebook ... and the family was keen, and I just thought, 'Oh, no. I can't confuse these two worlds'." Robert kept Facebook entirely for family and old school friends, although he did mix professional and personal posts on a blog he maintained.

Mark, who worked in marketing, deliberately limited his social network platforms to Facebook (for social interactions) and LinkedIn (for business interactions), avoiding Twitter entirely, on the basis of having limited time and resources. He explained that "you need to have the boundaries in social media". He managed his links with students very carefully, only connecting them with his contacts when he adjudged them to have enough maturity to have a professional narrative. At the same time, though, he appreciated the serendipitous connections that LinkedIn, in particular, made possible.

While LinkedIn was used by some of our participants, in particular those in marketing, for professional networking purposes, many others seemed bemused by it. Jen, for instance, was on LinkedIn but didn't use it, and was confused when family used it to contact her. Josh had joined LinkedIn as part of a job search process, but didn't understand why people he didn't know tried to link to him, "and you think, well, I've never met you, I've never worked with you – why would you be interested?" Dolly had had to join it to provide students with recommendations through its references portal, but was frustrated by the subsequent communications he received which he found completely irrelevant; if he needed to contact anyone in his field, he would do so by other means. James had a policy of not connecting with students or people he did not know, to avoid conflicts of interest; but, like Mark, he was happy to keep in touch with students on LinkedIn after their graduation. Managing the etiquette of these new kinds of social contacts was a challenge that our participants were figuring out largely independently as they went along.

Annie's use of social media was particularly mixed. She kept a personal research blog, a second blog for a research group she was involved in, was a regular tweeter for several group Twitter accounts – her department (in social sciences), a professional association, two research groups – and had a personal Twitter account, which she described as "a bit of a hybrid mix of, 'Here's something I found funny. Here is something I'm outraged about. Here's something professional.' It's a very eclectic mix of things". She also used Facebook for personal reasons, including using Messenger to deal with certain personal issues at work; she felt this more informal medium was useful, particularly in the case of dealing with very sensitive problems.

Departmental or school Twitter feeds were fairly common. There was often a division of labour here, with one person in a department being the point of contact for material to be posted on the departmental Twitter or Facebook page – sometimes an enthusiastic academic who might be designated "publicity rep" or "digital ambassador", sometimes a member of administrative staff or an intern with some hours of their workload explicitly designated for social media engagement. Natalie was one of our academic participants who had adopted this role in her department, controlling the history department blog, Twitter, and Facebook feeds. She had taken it upon herself to update the blog, putting it on a WordPress platform "because we hadn't quite achieved 21st century web presence yet", and appreciated the need to post on this regularly, both herself and from other members of the department, to "keep advertising what we're up to at all times". The level of engagement with and understanding of social media she showed, particularly in her reference to "21st century web presence", was unusual amongst our participants.

Where there was a designated social media person, material for online publication would usually be emailed to them for circulation. Don, for instance, said "I use the department's Twitter account, they're always asking for contributions ... I send them tweets quite regularly". Mark deliberately worked with the young social media intern in his department particularly to produce information aimed at students, feeling they were more likely to read something coming from her, rather than himself, as she is "young and relevant".

Not all of our participants were clearly aware of or engaged with this process, though. Verity knew that there was a departmental Twitter feed but did not engage with it: "We will talk about it, and if somebody else does it we thank the person who does it." Holly pointed out particular issues arising from her role as a part-time administrator:

> I did start thinking about tweeting, because obviously with a smartphone I could do that from wherever I am. I've kind of pulled back from that now. It's a boundary thing – it's hard to say, "I'm only going to tweet on Tuesdays, Wednesdays and Fridays". You know, that's not realistic. And of course, once you're on Twitter, you're then following other people and stuff is coming in and the phone's going "beep-beep-beep" all the time. I have enough on my plate without all that.

It was common for our participants to feel that their institution was encouraging engagement with social media in principle, though this was often expressed in quite general terms. Juliette provided an account of her recent decision to join Twitter, when a couple of people in her department began to use it and she started to feel what she described as "a slight pressure" to start using it herself. Will described "a general feeling that we should". He had received the occasional email from his department prompting him to think about public engagement through social media, but with no explicit directive; the decision was left to the individual. Diane described her decision to join Twitter as having been influenced only by "a bit of pull from students", combined with having seen a colleague begin to tweet who found that it did not require a great deal of extra work.

However, departments and institutions did not generally have more specific strategies about how to use social media, and most people were given the freedom to make their own decisions about this. As James said, "The social media stuff tends to boil down to, 'Be careful of your online presence because you represent the institution', the usual cautionary stuff". Phil, a head of department, described a simple departmental social media strategy "where we encourage people to re-tweet each other's tweets and raise our profile". He also made sure public profile was one of the topics discussed at probation and appraisal meetings. Simple as this may sound, it was more elaborate than most departments' positions. Stephanie, another head of department, felt it would be inappropriate to force people to engage, and so her department did not have a policy on social media. Occasionally, she had asked people not to say things publicly on Twitter or Facebook that might be problematic for the institution, for instance complaining about marking or student pressure. But she felt that, over time, most people had become more savvy and cautious, so decisions about what to put online were normally best left to individuals.

In some ways it is surprising that individuals are still given so much latitude around social media engagement, in contrast with the way in which public profiles are controlled on university websites. Academics' online self-representations contribute to the reputation of their institution, particularly in the contemporary context of heightened competition discussed in Chapter 1, and are therefore important for institutional strategy in the marketised university. International league tables in particular, such as the QS World University Rankings, place a great deal of weight on scholars' and departments' reputations. In this context, a strong public social media presence (combined with good publications of course) could serve as a useful reputation booster. Moreover, new technologies such as Altmetric (www.altmetric.com) make it increasingly possible to quantify and valorise online interaction, drawing it into the web of evaluation of research and impact that enfolds academic work. Some institutions do recognise this explicitly, at least in relation to specific platforms. For instance, Robert, a professor of maths from a prestigious research-intensive university, told us that the university actively encouraged involvement with Google Scholar, presumably to maximise the positive influence of Google Scholar rankings in the various league tables in which this was one of the quantified metrics. Ian, a mathematics lecturer at a different research-intensive university, had heard that some departments at his institution were either making a social media profile mandatory or were strongly encouraging one; but he felt that maths would be one of the last areas where this would be likely to happen, "not because of any innate rebelliousness of mathematicians, but just because we're very used to working on our own".

## Attitudes to using social media

For our academic participants, social media offers many new possibilities for communication between themselves, the rest of their field, and the wider world. This brings both trepidation and excitement, and our participants expressed a range of perspectives. Some embrace it, teaching themselves to blog and tweet regularly about their work as it developed, for both academic and non-academic audiences. Some felt the need to wait until their academic work was clearly established before making anything public on social media. Others refused to engage with social media at all. As Ian said, "Some people are really into it, and others just don't see the value of that".

Some people procrastinated or expressed confusion or a lack of understanding, rather than making an explicit decision not to engage. Andy, for instance, described his use of social media as very limited, arguing that "at the end of the day you will be linked with lots of people who are your friends, but not really your friends". He made what he called a "not very active" use of LinkedIn and ResearchGate and had "create Google Scholar and Research ID profile" on his to-do list. So, while he had a sense of the potential usefulness of some of these networks for his professional life, they had not yet reached the level of priority for him to actually sign up to them. Connor, likewise, as a head of department, approached social media "with caution". Gareth told us, "I don't understand the logic of any of that at a personal level or even, necessarily, at a work level". David said, "I don't necessarily approve of Twitter and Facebook, so I tend to avoid them". Valerie found that if someone tried to engage with her via Twitter, "I get in a vague state of panic … because I just don't feel comfortable with it. It still feels very new for me".

Others expressed resistance to social media in strong and decisive terms. Katherine explained that her department (marketing) had made a conscious decision not to use Facebook because many older members of the department didn't use it, adding that, on a personal level, "I must admit, I hate it with a passion … As far as I'm concerned, I'm in contact with all the people I want to be in contact with". Rebecca said, "I absolutely refuse to involve myself in any social networking. So, no, I haven't sent a tweet". She did engage with comments pages on news items relevant to her work, but was more comfortable sending letters to newspapers and writing articles than writing on social media. Dolly said, "I have an utter aversion to social media. Utter and complete". However, neither of these historians, despite their strong antipathy, were completely divorced from all forms of social media engagement. Dolly's research institute had a Twitter account, usually run by postgraduate students (consonant with the description of the division of labour above), and they did occasionally request him to provide them with a tweet – though he underlined that "they'll post it. I wouldn't go anywhere near posting it, or anything like that". And while Rebecca rejected social media in general, she had kept a blog while working on an upcoming book.

To some extent, these differences in levels of engagement may be related to age and career stage. Earlier in their career, academics are more likely to be seeking employment and to be trying to establish a reputation, so may use online writing to create and manage their digital presence. This can be empowering for those who have not yet produced a body of more formal scholarly work. Younger academics may also have a better sense of how to engage in this context. Chris, a head of department in history, found it fascinating, when sitting on appointments panels, to hear younger scholars discuss the need for outreach on blogs and social media. He felt PhD students kept some of the best academic blogs. Some older colleagues might still see this as "dumbing down", but these older colleagues would not necessarily be capable of blog-writing themselves: "It is actually a skill. I think there is an awareness of a different kind of audience, a different kind of mode of communication."

However, at the same time, the visibility necessarily associated with social media use can lead to self-doubt (Bennett & Folley, 2014, p. 6). Younger academics in particular may still be formulating their ideas and thus feel less confident about committing them to the internet, where everything they write will be subjected to bibliometrics and recorded for posterity; or they may feel their profile needs to be better established before making it public. Emma, an early career academic, explained that the reason she had not engaged with academic networking sites like academia.edu and ResearchGate was "because I'm too ashamed to be on there without any publications ... once I actually have some kind of published profile I will be on things like academia.edu and all the rest". Older academics may feel that social media is really for a different generation. Jamie, who had long experience in a previous job of engaging with traditional broadcast media and was skilled and comfortable with communicating with general audiences, was nevertheless resistant to extending this to online settings, saying, "I haven't mastered blogging yet, I'm afraid. I am being encouraged and I'm kind of trying to avoid it".

## Advantages and possibilities of social media

The diversity of perspectives described above among our participants reflects the different weightings they give to the perceived advantages and disadvantages of engagement with social media. Advantages included the possibilities opened up by social media for strategic, career-oriented purposes, such as highlighting their publications to increase citations (as Terras, 2012, discusses in her blog); networking with other academics and sharing resources (described in Veletsianos, 2012); communicating with new audiences; experimenting with and developing writing; and learning about and trying out new ways of teaching. Disadvantages included the additional time social media requires; the new kinds of engagement with the audience it opens up; the focus intrinsic to social media on the self, in addition to (or sometimes instead of) "the work"; and feelings of lack of control and additional risk.

Some among our participants deliberately started using social media for very targeted strategic purposes. Don, for instance, set up his Facebook account "with the explicit purpose of using it to publicise a book that I'd written for a trade readership", and also used Twitter to advertise his books. He was pleased to report that his book had been called "brilliant" in a conversation with a Twitter celebrity political pundit. This had led to a lot of retweets and publicity, and he felt that this had "made me more visible among academics", including those beyond his discipline. Likewise, Jen set up a Facebook page for the sole purpose of promoting a book, and Colin did the same on Twitter. Diane used Twitter to promote a special issue of a journal which she had edited. Natalie explained that her colleagues blog about their most recent articles, adding to what she described as a "very active writing culture" in their department. Personal strategic purposes may come into play, too. Charles was aware that in relation to social media, "some days you have to push it, like coming up to promotions committee".

As highlighted earlier, communication with new kinds of audiences, quickly and effectively, was another of the reasons people cited for starting to use social media. Charles had been considering signing up to Twitter, "purely because of the extent of the reach that you have". Rory saw blogs as a potential means of dissemination to a wider audience, particularly in the context of gaining visibility when bidding for funding. Andy was planning to set up a personal research website, for a very specific audience of potential PhD students and postdocs. Jen explained that she had started using a combination of Twitter and Facebook when she was advertising and running a MOOC (Massive Open Online Course) and wanted to advertise it to a wide range of people. While she felt that this had been a very useful strategy, enabling her to reach out to larger audiences, she thought that otherwise social media was "a waste of time".

Twitter, in particular, offered people a combination of potentially large audiences and a relatively non-intrusive approach, particularly as compared to other modes of communication like mass emails. As Annie explained,

> if they're not interested, they can stop following you. The power is in their hands ... It feels a lot less invasive to do it via Twitter and the potential audience is much bigger, and also if people retweet, it amplifies the signal that much more.

Twitter also enables a mix of academic and more personal contact. Don felt that "I think sometimes the purpose of the Twitter account is to show that we are real human beings. So if, for example, we win a pub quiz, I usually send that".

While research and public engagement-related communication predominated in social media engagement for most of our participants, a few of our participants and their colleagues were also using social media as part of their teaching activities, or for communicating with students. Katherine, an administrator in a marketing department, described how her teaching colleagues were inviting students to interact on a Twitter feed which fed into the Moodle site for their module. The lecturers then observed these discussions and could draw on them in planning their next lectures. Ella and Simon, academics in different disciplines (history and marketing), both had Facebook groups set up for their main undergraduate courses in which they addressed students' questions, but also discussed course content, like posting relevant news items or memes for response.

One final possibility which some of our participants raised was that some people were benefiting from engaging with the new genres associated with social media in developing their own writing. Rose, head of a marketing department, felt that outlets like *The Conversation* (a professionally edited academic blog) and Twitter led people to think differently about how to say what they want to, and to be more aware of different possibilities: "That makes people talk about writing differently. People say, 'I've got to write this in a certain tone of voice'."

Collin, an academic in history, discussed this potential for improving writing at some length, saying, "I suspect what's going on is a lot of the active bloggers are also active in terms of writing their research up into articles, because they're learning to write". He described a colleague who has been blogging for years who blogs about "anything; he blogs about teaching, he blogs about research, he blogs about politics, and you can't say he doesn't do anything else, because he's writing at the same time". Note the distinction Collin makes here between "blogging" and "writing", by which he clearly means "research-related writing for publication". Seeing this advantage of regular blogging, he was planning to encourage his students to blog, to develop what he called "good writing, coherent writing, writing that speaks perhaps to an audience other than your immediate circle of friends". We see here how the advantage described above of engaging with different audiences is both an intrinsic advantage in itself and potentially contributes to writing development.

In summary, those of our participants who did engage with social media were usually quite ready to identify the reasons why they found this a useful thing to do and, more generally, the advantages and possibilities offered by this new space, in terms of strategic possibilities, engaging with new audiences, providing new ways to approach teaching, and developing their writing. However, alongside these advantages and possibilities, tensions and difficulties were identified which could make engagement with social media a double-edged sword.

## Challenges associated with social media

Engaging with social media has costs, in addition to benefits, particularly in terms of the time and effort it takes to follow other researchers or to maintain one's own online presence. There may be cognitive costs involved in sorting and filtering the huge amount of information online (Carrigan, 2015a). It may be experienced as distracting, even by those who enjoy such forms of scholarship (Bennett & Folley, 2014). There is a cost of time and effort associated with learning anything new, and new genres may not be well understood by people whose training and experience is in an entirely different kind of writing. For example, in a blog post, Cortez (2013) describes blogging as primarily a form of discussion, but claims that many academics attempt to read blog posts as though they were papers or opinion pieces. Acquiring and engaging with digital scholarship practices takes time that many academics feel they do not have, particularly when such practices may not be perceived as "real work" (Leon & Pigg, 2011, p. 3).

In terms of the values attached to different types of writing, it is incontrovertible that more academic capital can be achieved by publishing extensively in the traditional academic genres of monograph and (especially) journal article, particularly in the context of the pressure to become adequately REF-able discussed earlier. When academics are making choices about their writing, there is a need to balance engagement with social media with spending time doing other types of writing which might be more highly valued or achieve particular aims. As Charles put it, "At the end of the day, it doesn't matter how good your blog is, you've got to deliver on your papers".

While Dolly thought that blogs were interesting in principle, he also felt that the specific audience and value associated with a more traditional route for academic public communication mattered a great deal more than the wider audiences a blog might reach. Referring to an article he'd written for *Times Higher Education*, he said he would rather write for this forum than write a blog post, because it is "read by the Vice-Chancellors ... Those are the people I want to influence".

The issue of the time available for writing in general, and the need to prioritise the types of writing which are most highly valued, is a particularly important one, reflecting the time pressures discussed in Chapter 4. Don, a historian, said that while he would be pleased when things were retweeted, and appreciated his postgraduate student's engagement with Twitter, he had no personal interest in tweeting regularly himself: "I think it's a bit of a waste of time. I'm so busy with other things, I can't be doing that." Verity, a senior academic close to retirement, was putting off engagement on social media until that point, because of the email pressures discussed in the previous chapter (and note her use of the "bombardment" metaphor): "At the moment I think email is enough to deal with. Every day I'm bombarded by masses of messages." Similarly, Alex said that while he had wondered about getting a Facebook account, he felt that "I just don't want any more electronic inputs in my life". He tweeted occasionally and found it a good way of keeping up with his field, but recognised the cost of it too, as "another mode of distraction"; since "email looms so large, I just think I don't want another stream of information distracting me". Robyn struggled to find the time to maintain the information even on her departmental personal website, "because I have other priorities and it's such an administrative thing to do to actually sit down and put that information on the website", let alone interacting on other professional social media like LinkedIn and ResearchGate, sites which she had a presence on but did not have time to maintain.

Valerie told us she had recently committed in a research grant bid to writing and maintaining blogs if the research were funded. She was aware that "it's really important to engage in that way", but after going to a training session on using blogs and social media, she was shocked at the time commitment it entailed: "it almost felt like another massive layer on top of the activities that you're already doing". Her strength of feeling about this is captured in the way she spoke about her response: "it fills me with horror, it really does".

James was wary about what he called "social media in the traditional sense, the Facebook, Twitter, Flickr side of things", because of their potential for proliferation. Again, this was set in relation to other demands: "I only have a limited amount of time. I can't monitor everything, and I'm not interested in monitoring all that stuff." He was also increasingly concerned about his "digital footprint". Even when he did engage in relation to personal interests such as commenting on news articles about the sports team he followed, he would carefully anonymise his responses. For Andy, Facebook had proved to be "just completely annoying and wasting the majority of my free time"; after his first couple of months on it, he had stopped using it entirely.

Managing colleagues' willingness to engage with social media under time pressure was an even greater pressure. Clara, as a head of department, was very enthusiastic about the possibilities of social media in her context, and as mentioned above, her department had allocated workload hours to a colleague, Natalie, to tweet and to keep a blog. They had ambitious plans for the blog, including both publicising research and impact and engagement, and more student-facing work, writing up field trips and reflecting on learning. Colleagues in the department were invited to submit the blog, but they recognised the need to manage this around academics' workloads and made these requests at quieter times of year.

Natalie's engagement with the departmental Facebook and Twitter accounts came with its own temporal challenges. She invested a significant amount of time in this daily, and this was reflected in her departmental workload commitment. "To maintain the kind of traffic that our department needs for that Twitter account to be successful I check in with Twitter two to three times a day for ten to twenty minutes, do retweets, do notifications." In contrast, she did not have workload hours allocated to maintain her own personal social media accounts, and found these tended to become neglected, which caused her some concern: "The fact that I am not able to maintain mine actually does have some long-term effects on my ability to disseminate my research, which is a bit frustrating."

Engaging with new platforms is costly not only in relation to the time taken to actually write, but also in the demands of solving technical challenges which can arise. Diane had set up a blog site on WordPress. She was initially very enthusiastic, receiving great feedback on her blog posts from colleagues and considering turning them into a book. She invested time and effort into crafting her blog posts, and the blog became "quite an important thing about me understanding myself and my unfolding research". But then the server hosting the blog was hit by a virus. She was sent complex information about how to fix it using updates and patches but found that "I don't have time to fix the virus, because I don't know how to fix viruses". So, the blog became inaccessible to readers and was lying dormant, a source of disappointment to her but not something she had the time or money to invest in re-awakening.

In addition to time pressures, the nature of the engagement with the audience on social media has its own challenges, such as a loss of control over what happens to work once it is published online. The audience for online writing such as blog posts and tweets is more diffuse than that for traditional genres such as the monograph or journal article, making it more challenging for a writer to anticipate the readership's needs, interests, and responses. Responses to any kind of social media engagement can be quickly and easily posted by anyone. This can lead to people's views being misrepresented or misused, or even make people subject to attack. This is a particular risk for women and minority groups, who tend to experience more harassment online (Lupton, 2014).

The kinds of responses our participants received from broader audiences differed in scale, scope, and timing, from the kinds of responses they would have expected from traditional academic audiences. The simple volume of responses could be intimidating on its own. Collin explained that "Twitter can make you feel persecuted because you log on and you've got 50 new tweets". But lack of engagement from audiences could also be unsettling. Rebecca, for example, had attempted to engage people in discussions on her monograph-related blog, but was disappointed to discover that "it wasn't successful, it didn't attract people to it".

As well as a general sense of overwhelm or loss of control of audience response, more direct attacks can also be a risk. Dolly had been involved in what he described as "a Twitter storm" related to a conference he was organising, in which the choice of speakers had been extensively critiqued, first in a private letter, and then in an open letter published on Twitter, which generated a great deal of debate. He had refused to engage with this directly, as he felt the critiques both had been answered and were without foundation, but still felt that "it's just a disgrace … Basically what happens is lots of people who don't know what's going on start commenting on what you do. And that's what social media's about". On the basis both of this experience and of his general observations, he described social media as being "about witch hunting, at the end of the day. Social media is about people who actually don't do research, just sitting there carping at the sidelines".

The immediacy of the timescales of social media responses can prove challenging, both in terms of speed of responses and the rate at which interest moves on. Mick found that his use of social media with students, including setting up a WhatsApp group, had raised expectations that he would be available "24/7/365" so he had started to scale back on this. Dolly described a Twitter response as being "like a balloon, you blow it up and immediately, because the media move on so quickly, there's a pin in it and it's gone". Natalie felt that for a blog to be successful, "you really do need to be publishing something new, at a minimum once a month, but ideally every ten days. For any academic I don't think that's feasible, so you're just never going to get ... a really successful blog unless you're extraordinarily prolific". This pressure for speedy publication and response is quite different from the very slow timescales often associated with both publication of and response to academic work. As Collin said, "You want to think that the lifetime of your work is not counted in weeks or months, but in years".

Another subtle, but important, difference between traditional academic writing and social media platforms comes in the orientation they have to the representation of the self. Social media highlights the self as an individual, rather than simply the work. It is seen by some as trivial or self-aggrandising (Lupton, 2013) for this reason. The key tension, for some of our participants, came not in making their research work public but in this self-promotion associated with social media. Brian described Facebook as being "like a shop window", and said he was uncomfortable with it, not wanting to "put [my]self out like that". He didn't mind having a professional or a research profile made public, but "I don't like it as a life thing, really". Charles spoke at length about finding social media inappropriately self-indulgent:

> I find it a bit me, me, I, I ... Was it Abraham Lincoln once said, "It's better to remain silent and for everybody to assume that you're a fool than to open your mouth and confirm the fact" ... The tweeting, you don't want to be known as the James Blunt of academia, where it's too easy to tweet about bloody anything.

Charles here orients to social norms of politeness and good behaviour in which one avoids self-praise. "I think it probably goes back to how I've been brought up ... It's nice for you to say nothing and for people to be pleasantly surprised." Josh, similarly, described blogs as "self-indulgent" and felt that Twitter was characterised by trivia, "too many people telling people what they've had for tea". Gareth said "I seriously don't get it, at a personal level. I'd rather let my output speak for themselves rather than anything else, at a work level". Emma, an early career researcher, as we mentioned above saw online engagement activities as being potentially used from what she called "a brand awareness point of view", interpreting building her own academic career and visibility in terms drawn from marketing theory, but was unwilling to do much of this until she had built up a portfolio of more traditional academic publications.

On the other hand, Diane had a different, less individualistic interpretation. She felt that the training courses she'd seen advertised rather misunderstood Twitter, by highlighting the self-publicity angle. She saw Twitter as much more a space to make connections with people interested in the same phenomena or theoretical constructs that she was, by creating what she called "a trail that's of interest to them, as it is to me".

## Conclusion: professional identity and future implications

This chapter has demonstrated the diversity of ways in which academics engage with social media in their writing lives. The wide range of social media now available opens up many exciting new possibilities for engagement with new audiences, in new ways, developing new genres, and some academics take these possibilities up enthusiastically. However, social media activities also bring costs and risks: they take time (which, as we have seen in Chapter 4, is often experienced as precious, limited, and to be protected); they require investment in learning new platforms and practices; and as well as their potential for reputational enhancement, they can also be associated with reputational risks. It is perhaps not surprising, therefore, that, at this point in time, responses from our participants around social media were so diverse, from keen engagement to outright rejection.

It seems likely that, over time, expectations for academics to have an active social media presence will grow, while more explicit norms will develop around social media presence and practices. If the findings from our earlier chapters continue to apply in this arena, these norms may well end up being shaped by disciplinary knowledge traditions, as well as being framed within managerial pressures and expectations. For now, though, the kind of online identity academics can choose to develop remains at least one arena in which individual choice remains fairly open. The stance an academic adopts towards engagement with social media depends ultimately on the kind of scholar they aspire to be and the kinds of audiences they want to engage with.

It is clear from the discussions above that one of the key strengths of social media in the academic professional sphere is for networking and to facilitate collaboration with peers. Relationships and writing collaborations have always been important in scholarly work, but the tools, technologies, and media now available have opened up many new ways in which such relationships can be facilitated. In the next chapter we move on to address the importance of relationships and collaboration in academics' writing practices.

# 8

# RELATIONSHIPS AND COLLABORATION IN ACADEMIC WRITING

## Introduction

We have seen in Chapter 7 how social media can facilitate collaboration among academics. The current chapter looks more closely at this workplace collaboration, the relationships that sustain it, and the place of relationships in academics' writing lives across their research, teaching, administrative, and service roles. In line with the situated social practice perspective outlined in Chapters 1 and 2, we see knowledge and learning as effects of situated activity within networks of relationships. Writing activities in universities occur within discourse communities that share labour, and these divisions of labour also mediate text production, as do a number of less direct sponsors of literacy (Park & De Costa, 2015), including political and economic forces such as internationalisation, managerialism, and digitisation.

The internationalisation of higher education means that new skills and practicalities are involved in collaborating with research colleagues and teams across time zones, physical spaces, and languages. The role of English as a lingua franca in higher education was not much discussed by our participants, the majority of whom had English as a first language. However, this is an important strand of debate in relation to equity in international academic networks (see Lillis & Curry, 2006; Cardenas & Rainey, 2018). The influence of managerialism is reflected in increased focus on accountability and demonstrating excellence in teaching, which leaves its mark on the relationships that are encouraged between academics and the various communities they engage with, including students. Finally, digitisation has brought greater opportunities for collaborative writing, while at the same time privileging certain types of literacy practices (Wargo & De Costa, 2017), and influencing who engages with whom in writing relationships.

This chapter focuses on the ways in which writing practices are shared with colleagues across disciplines and institutions, and across role boundaries, such as writing shared with administrative and technical colleagues. First, we discuss how relationships in research writing are established and maintained before turning to the ways in which teaching and feedback-related writing tasks are shared among colleagues and how technology impacts on relationships between staff and students. Finally, we explore how divisions of labour around administrative writing have shifted over time, and how relationship building can be central to administrative and service writing.

## Sharing in research writing

Although scholarly writing is often characterised as a solitary activity, a central aspect of almost all the research writing in this study was the importance of relationships. Our informants described working with others on research-related texts such as journal articles, conference papers, and grant applications. Even where these were ostensibly sole-authored, they still entailed working with colleagues such as editors, conference organisers, and administrative staff. Many of our participants spoke about how fruitful and enjoyable it was to work on research writing with colleagues. For example, Charles and Lisa both described the pleasures of meeting colleagues in person to work on research writing together:

> I find it's much better to do stuff face to face than over Skype or on the phone. I'm driving to [City name] tonight and to a lesser or greater extent it's sometimes the only fun you have. You know, work should be fun and sometimes it isn't ... I don't find it is a solitary process, I find it very much convivial with other co-authors.
>
> *(Charles)*

> A lot of the time we do try to work together on it [a research article], coming face to face, because I think that does actually help. You can brainstorm, you can bounce around ideas. Also we'll read it out together and decide before we put something in whether or not it's absolutely perfect. Each sentence gets deconstructed. We're quite a good team that way.
>
> *(Lisa)*

This communal process of going through a text together line by line was described by several of our participants, and was associated with the pleasures of friendship and intellectual debate. Being in the same room as others and discussing research ideas face to face appears to play an important role in building social relationships. There was acknowledgement that digital platforms such as email, Skype, and file-sharing software had changed things in this regard, facilitating more and faster collaborative writing, as we have seen already in Chapter 6. Marketing lecturer Mark, for example, said, "We can speak to people in real time all of the time, which is great, academically". While digitisation was widely acknowledged to have made collaboration across time and space more feasible, Robert also noted that it had changed the nature of his working patterns:

> We'd sit down and we'd go through that line by line together. Now we use the technology if you like to allow us to disappear off, do little bits and come back and exchange that in a sensible way … It's certainly true that the friendships were, in a sense, more intense then. You were sitting round and everyone was trying to put in their tuppence and choose – A lot of talking and arguing but in a positive way. It was just great fun. Writing became this activity that you did with others in the room. It's tended to be much more now that you capture the ideas and then somebody goes off and does a first draft and other people comment on it.

This represents a shift from what Ryberg, Davidsen, and Hodgson (2017) describe as truly "collaborative" work, involving face-to-face discussion, towards greater use of "cooperative" working patterns, in which people work individually on their allocated parts of a task. The latter has not entirely replaced the former, but has enabled more efficient sharing of information between meetings and, arguably, decreased the intensity of collaborative writing. Digital platforms also allow academics to keep in touch and maintain "togetherness" (Ryberg et al., 2017) while working separately. In this sense relationships continue to play a pivotal role even in forms of writing that are, prima facie, solo endeavours. Although, as Robert notes above, co-authors can comment electronically on each other's writing, for some, meeting face-to-face and engaging in practices such as reading text aloud was important for establishing an appropriate shared "voice" in the writing.

While certain aspects of research work are facilitated by digital technology, this may not apply to all types of intellectual work. For instance, Menzies and Newson (2007) argue that although instant communication is facilitated by email and other technologies, online communication does not facilitate engagement in in-depth, critical thinking, dialogue, or participatory knowledge creation. An account is given of work on a book done by email which was delayed for three years, until an extended period of face-to-face work was organised. "Email made it possible for us to work together, but somehow it didn't help us get the work done" (Menzies & Newson, 2007, p. 91). This view appears to find some support in Charles' comment above about the benefits of meeting face-to-face rather than relying on Skype or phone. Menzies and Newson suggest that this shift from collaboration to cooperation has important implications both for knowledge creation and for society as a whole.

With regard to how these collaborative relationships were established in the first place, several participants mentioned the importance of relationships with literacy brokers (Lillis & Curry, 2006) such as friends and colleagues that they had known for some time. For early career academics in particular, continuing relationships with PhD supervisors were often influential. Asked which colleagues she had the most contact with, Robyn explained:

> I would say probably mostly with my former PhD supervisor, because he's the person whose interests are closer to mine, so he usually has a lot of PhD students, so they give talks and I'm usually part of those sessions.

For younger academics who have not yet been able to build up an extensive network for research collaborations, their PhD supervisors can be a source of fruitful co-authoring relationships, as illustrated by Mark's comment:

> My own experience is that they don't seem to be interested in that level here. They don't have the interest in many of the topic areas, so you tend to develop writing partnerships with other people at other universities, just because that's where you're being supervised, and they're the people you've been used to.

The role of these relationships can also extend beyond the mediation of text production and into broader mentorship on one's overall development as an academic, as was the case for Rory:

> So for example, my PhD supervisors, they were really, really good because they didn't necessarily just give me a supervision on PhDs, they gave me a supervision on how to be an academic, if you like.

However, it is fair to say that the continuing importance of relationships with supervisors post-PhD, and particularly co-authorship with supervisors, was not consistent across our data. This is likely to be influenced both by different disciplinary expectations and by the specificities of supervisory relationships.

Newer relationships for research work were in some cases established by means of sharing work online. One maths lecturer, Brian, had established three groups on LinkedIn to discuss research and share work in progress, and was surprised at the number of people who wanted to join them quite quickly. Academics have always participated in disciplinary networks, but the gradual shift towards "social scholarship" (Greenhow & Gleason, 2014), in which social networking is part of the research, writing, and publishing process, has amplified the need for connectedness, as illustrated by Don's use of social media to publicise his work:

I first set up a Facebook account in about 2012 with the explicit purpose of using it to publicise a book that I'd written for a trade readership and I think I started using Twitter at about the same time simply to try and publicise the book and to increase its sales.

As well as existing relationships and online networking, locality and shared research interests also act as drivers for the development of relationships around research. A critical mass of interested local colleagues could drive the direction that research took over time, leading to the development of a centre of expertise, as described by David:

So [a colleague] was always interested in that area and wanted to continue that work when he went to this university. Managed to organise it in that way and that's now continued. You do need a certain number of people who are a core group.

Another means of establishing writing relationships was via networking at conferences, and a sense of solidarity among academics facing similar challenges or at a similar career stage could be established even across physical distances, as shown in this comment by Emma:

I have just met at a conference two other women actually, as it happens, who are at the very same career stage as me. We all finished our PhDs within six months of each other. And part of the conference was a round table discussion, and there is a special issue that we've decided to try and pull a paper together on. So we've had our first Skype call, because we're not local, about what we're going to do.

These findings on the role of relationships in research writing suggest something of a shift from fewer, more intense relationships around truly collaborative writing (Ryberg et al., 2017), towards more diffuse relationships characterised by cooperative working, whereby new relationships around writing can be established and maintained fairly quickly with the aid of digital technology.

## Teaching collaborations

Relationships with students are obviously central to the teaching process, although collaborations between academics, other colleagues, and support staff of various kinds are also involved. As noted above, these relationships are changing in important respects as more, and more diverse, students enter the system through internationalisation and marketisation of higher education and through the increasing reach and efficiency of digital technologies which have increased the potential of online teaching and communication. One of the major consequences of rising student numbers in the UK is an increase in teaching loads and associated paperwork for academics, and this can, in Brandt's (1998) terms, "suppress" higher-status forms of literacy by undermining opportunities for scholarly writing. The frustrations of this tension between teaching and research writing is seen in the following comments by lecturers Jen and Emma:

> Also you need to know your teaching load. This autumn, my teaching load was really high. I kind of deliberately made the decision not to plan to write anything because then it just makes me quite anxious, frustrated, and I don't have enough time to write.
>
> *(Jen)*

> Well, I think the challenges that I have faced, past tense, have been around balancing workload … I had quite a heavy teaching load, because we've got a new workload model in place … where workload means points, and if you're not over a certain level of points you don't get paid for additional work. I had done the additional work, and was under the points, so I had to boost my teaching. Yes, last year was really busy, and I struggled to do more than a day a week on my [research].
>
> *(Emma)*

A high teaching load usually brings with it the task of assessing student work and providing feedback on it. The amount and diversity of written feedback to students was important in our data and prompted responses across the whole spectrum from being seen as a creative challenge to being experienced as drudgery and distraction. A large amount of time is spent on giving feedback, and sometimes digital technologies such as Turnitin and processes of electronic feedback increase rather than decrease the demands, as Natalie explains:

> Everything gets marked through Turnitin. I suppose that's quite extensive in terms of writing time, I spent three or four days the week before last, during reading week, marking. We have a particular set of criteria: argument, knowledge, presentation style, those sorts of things, all of which require a sort of 200 or 300 word blurb in addition to the comments you've actually given on the original paper, which is actually much more extensive than the amount of marking I was doing at [another university], where I was previously, where you marked in a Word document and then wrote a very short blurb back to students. Marking a Word document was a lot easier as well.

Again, a move towards standardisation in marking and feedback is evident in the practices used in Natalie's department, and such practices tended to be commented on less favourably than giving feedback directly to students. In Bob's comment below, he notes positive aspects of this approach, but also points to negative changes in the nature of the relationship between staff and students:

> the three-line whip now that as of last year all marking has to be done electronically and feedback given electronically, either through Grade-Mark or another way. Personally, I quite like GradeMark. I quite like using it. You can adapt it. I can use it on my iPad, do it on the train or whatever. But it does bring in another level of bureaucracy in some ways because, you know, before, you would sit down with a script, write on them and there you are, there's your essay back, you know, and in some ways you lose that personal contact with students in a way, to actually give them feedback on not just their writing but on their understanding of things.

The effect of their feedback on students was very important to academics, and several participants commented on the quality of interaction associated with different ways of providing feedback. For instance, Rose found voice recognition software helpful to enable her to convey her immediate responses as she read her students' work:

> I have Dragon voice recognition software ... that was absolutely fantastic for a certain type of writing. What I used it for was for "feedback on student work" writing. It was just the best. You're reading, and you're just saying what you're thinking as you're reading. Then, you've got a really lovely piece of writing for the students to read.

Wargo and De Costa (2017) include technologies in their definition of literacy sponsors, and while those who design or enforce the use of technologies such as Turnitin and GradeMark would undoubtedly argue that they are intended to support the provision of useful feedback, one could equally argue that, in privileging certain aspects of the feedback process, they regulate and exclude others such as individuality, creativity, and the development of the sort of personal connections with students that many academics value so highly. In our data, academics talk about their relationships with students warmly, seeing engagement with them as a rewarding and key part of their role and vocation:

> I would say the aspect that I enjoy most is teaching ... I think it comes more naturally to me than research, and I think I like the interaction with the students.

*(Robyn)*

I like the good sessions where you can see students really gaining something from the experience of being here.

*(Leonard)*

Arguably, increases in class sizes and the associated need to provide feedback and other information about courses efficiently to large numbers of students risk the loss of some of these valued and more personal aspects of relationships with students. Technologies are enabling sponsors of literacy in certain respects, facilitating communication en masse, but bringing with them changes in relationships between academics and their students.

## Administrative writing

Administrative writing included course handbooks, module descriptors, validation documents, minutes and agendas for meetings, and, of course, the many types of emails that are generated in order to share and co-ordinate work. Because much administrative work was passed between colleagues to write collectively, relationships played a significant role in this type of writing. This process brought our participants both pleasure and frustration. The nature of administrative writing and who was involved in its production were felt to have changed. Over the years, the division of labour has shifted between academics, administrators, and support staff such as technicians or financial specialists. For example, participants who had been working in academia for a long time described departmental secretaries typing up their PhD theses when they were students, like Gareth, who said:

I wrote it, all the way through the PhD, the first drafts were all written by hand. It was only after I'd cleaned them to; actually, what I viewed was the finished level, before any element of typing occurred. I didn't type those; the department secretary typed all of it. It was incredible. The chance of that nowadays is zero, isn't it?

Typing was not the only aspect of writing work where the distribution of roles had changed, however, and academics were often expected to take on roles that they did not have responsibility for in the past. Bob explained:

There's a lot changed in terms of how we interact with certain parts of the student's lifecycle, if you like. We are far more part of it in the induction process than we were. We're the ones who have to administer things like module registration.

Joe, a head of department in an area of management, was critical of the increased administrative workload associated with this expansion of the academic role. He felt that academics were responsible for everything now; not just teaching and research, but also administration, admissions, and marketing. Helping students learn seemed to have taken a back seat. He told us that he spends as much time as possible with students, and prioritises student emails, but finds most of his time is spent fulfilling administrative functions.

Andrew, another head of department, saw such trends as part of a more general worsening of the academic environment in the past 15 years. He identified a tension between his role as head and his underlying identity as a "mere academic". As head, his priority was to ensure that the department should become "a widely recognised, top ten department in the UK, both in teaching and research". But as an academic, being a successful department would mean, "everybody is satisfied with their position. Everybody has time to do their research. Everybody doesn't feel harried and forced to do various things that they don't want to do". He therefore faced conflicting pressures in his position, needing both to ensure the smooth running and strategic flourishing of the department, and to protect his staff from increased and unwelcome administrative demands.

The perception that academics were being given more administrative work to do was also shared by administrative staff such as Amanda, who worked in professional services:

> But in recent years, there seems to be more for them [academics] to do and not for us. I used to do student handbooks. I don't do them anymore. There's lots of things we don't do anymore. The rationale behind it, I don't know.

As touched on in Chapter 4, course handbooks may be subject to quality assurance processes and may be written using a template from previous years or other programmes. Such writing work involves collating and updating information from multiple sources and may require certain elements to be standardised across programmes. Although several people have contributed to a course handbook, the style is expected to be relatively uniform, as Jen explains:

> The handbook exists. This is like I've got a template that I just need to revise from one year to the other. Some of the things just simply mean changing the dates, changing key pieces of information such as our new REF result, ranking, new members of staff and so on. This year I had to go to the regulations because we'd got this standardised thing. I had to crosscheck what is already included and then copy and paste things or reformulate things. I didn't have to write it from scratch. When I wrote it from scratch, I was using another programme as a model.

Jen's comments illustrate the way text production is mediated by both political and material dimensions of literacy sponsorship of the type that stems from interactions between individuals in discourse communities (Prior, 1998; Swales, 1990). The former includes the broader marketisation of higher education in the UK, which pushes universities to compete for tuition fee income and market themselves in terms of rankings and means that data such as REF results and league table rankings become part of handbooks, prospectuses, and websites. We saw another potent example of how quality assurance processes can mediate texts in Chapter 3, when Don's approach to responses to external examiners' reports had to change in view of QAA requirements to make these responses public. The local socio-material aspects of literacy include divisions of labour within the institution, which constrain the writer's individual voice by imposing a degree of standardisation on the text. Standardisation of texts such as handbooks can impose challenges regarding the level of fit between the text, as a representative of an imagined reality, and the actual practices and constraints on the ground. The academics writing them may feel, as Diane does below, that the voice they are required to use does not "belong" to them:

> when you come to the handbook you have to go back and find where the hell was that article and then pull out those aims and then you have to think, "Okay, bear in mind the teaching team I've got on it, does that still work?" You have to think about the language that you want so you can get the ethos and culture of the programme right and then you have to bang that down everybody's throats so they get your vision.

This example, and much other administrative writing, is overseen at a distance by other "layers" of the university, as course descriptions have to pass through course validation committees and quality control systems of various sorts. Such texts can also often be generated by the demands of these distant layers, and in the case of professional training, by disciplinary organisations outside of the immediate university, which can make them feel both tedious and high-stakes – a lethal combination for job satisfaction. Mark describes writing a course validation document for a partner institution overseas:

> The documents, it started off last August, and the documents are absolutely huge. It's literally 150, 160 pages per document. Basically, you're working on a template which has been sent by the Educational Board, and you need to fill out the questions and answers. Then what happens is, it's submitted, then they want further clarification on points. So then you have to supply or create more documents to support the points they make … So that will then be appendix 2. So to put it into context, there is now a 220-page document, and we are on appendix A2. So I've gone round the alphabet, and I'm starting at A again, with A2.

In other cases, administrative staff, who had their own aims and preferences for such documents, would reformat text, sometimes in ways that reflected a different set of understandings of the text's purpose, as in Verity's example of transformations made to a draft constitution document by the school's head of administration:

> When I was head of school, like, an example would be working out a constitution, for the school, and that was kind of collaborative, but it was sort of a long, great big, document. I remember that the head of school administration then converted the great long document that I'd been organising, and largely writing, into one sheet with boxes. [Laughter] I was so amazed that sort of twelve to fifteen pages, of constitution, was suddenly rendered as a heap of boxes.

Although there was a perception among our participants that more administrative work had fallen to academics to do, administrative staff also appeared to be overloaded with work at times. Administrative staff talked about working in "teams of one" in which cutbacks meant that there was a lack cover for absence. As Fiona says:

> we unfortunately don't have enough cover. We don't work in teams where we've all got the same work, there aren't two or three people doing my workload. There is just me. There's only me that really knows what I'm doing.

Administrative support staff ended up shouldering extra work and working beyond their statutory hours, during holidays, sick leave, and weekends, particularly to catch up with emails:

> when I have been off ill, I sometimes come in on a Saturday, when it's quiet, just to, kind of, go through my emails and deal with a few things.
>
> *(Gillian)*

> If I'm not on my main two weeks holiday, then I will go onto my emails. Maybe I shouldn't have said that, but I will go onto my email.
>
> *(Amanda)*

These comments demonstrate that the problem described by academics in Chapter 4, of work, particularly checking and responding to emails, bleeding into personal time, affects everyone involved in the sharing of administrative work. Administrative and academic staff remain messily entangled in each other's working lives through the writing they share. This can work well, but breaks in the chain of communication can lead to time-wasting and frustration, as explained by administrator Sheena:

I think in terms of deadlines and maybe my colleague would say exam papers and exam marks and stuff like that, you know they are not always done at the time the admin staff would want them. But then we would say, "We need them in that time" and then the academics might say, "Well that was unrealistic", so there are potentially those clashes.

Administrative staff are heavily involved in pastoral work through their roles in admissions, attendance monitoring, and feeding back on student performance, and the fact that academics are often away and unable to respond as quickly as students might wish means that desperate emails are sent to admin staff, who feel a duty of care to respond:

Then we just get bombarded constantly by, "I've emailed that person, they haven't got back to me", and ... You know? It's not fair, because they do worry, and it's easier just to put that worry to bed than it is to let them just hang on, and hang on, and hang on.

*(Katherine)*

The ease of email communication may lead students to ask questions by email in cases where they might previously have visited the office in person. Likewise, they may tend to expect quick responses, not realising that their email is one among hundreds received that day. Furthermore, if students see themselves as paying customers, they might be more inclined to expect certain levels of "care", including rapid responses to queries. In these ways, the wider context of digitisation and commodification of higher education influences the relationships between students and staff, which in turn shape the writing practices that are shared among them.

## Writing in service relations

As described earlier, while participants' workloads were commonly divided into the three main components of research, teaching, and administration, there were some elements of academics' work that did not fall neatly into this workload allocation. These are the activities that we have called "service". This is made up of work that can be internal or external to the institution, and often goes beyond a person's job description but remains relevant to their academic identity. Internal service includes pastoral roles such as acting as dean of a college in institutions with a collegiate system, mentoring younger colleagues, and the general collegiality of attending events and supporting others' efforts. External service includes involvement with professional associations, research councils and grant-awarding bodies, government organisations, and committees; reviewing articles for journals; editorial publishing work; public engagement such as popular publishing, media appearances; external examining; and writing references for students and colleagues.

Service blurs with other categories, including internal administration and institutional decision-making, and "public engagement", which many senior academics in our study were involved with, and saw as part of their work role. Relationships played a significant role in this sort of work, since it was generally done out of a sense of community, often disciplinary community, and social responsibility. Maths professor Robert described happily participating in professional associations and writing popular books:

> I've been head of department. I'm also quite involved in professional organisations. I've been vice president of the [Professional Institute] and so there's a policy side of what I do as well. I also do popular maths things. I see that all as part of the same job.

There was also acknowledgement that this kind of service work is much more favourably regarded by universities now than it used to be, and although most of the senior academics in our study did engage with this sort of work, it was also acknowledged that not everyone saw service as part of their role. David asked:

> Do we ever see a job description of what the job entails? Of course, it's about the administration, a lot of research and teaching, mainly at post-graduate level. So those three activities. Beyond that, I think the job of professor is bigger than that. It's not just the institution, it's also keeping the whole system going through research councils, government organisations and sitting on committees. So that's part of it. Some people take that view, some people don't; I do. I guess some people enjoy these activities more than others too.

The ambiguity around whether or not service is part of an academic's job or not, and the ambivalence of some academics towards it, may stem from the fact that the very concept of service (for which academics usually do not get paid) is predicated on notions of collegiality and social responsibility. Many of our participants aligned themselves with this view of higher education as a public good (Naidoo & Williams, 2015), but nevertheless acknowledged that this is at odds with the neoliberal regime that academics in the UK work under, in which higher education is treated as a private good to be paid for by students and "delivered" by academics as service providers (Felt, Igelsböck, Schikowitz, & Völker, 2016).

## Conclusions

Rather than distracting from the work of writing, relationships with others were highly valued and central to the scholarly and teaching identities our participants held dear. Even where work such as writing feedback could cause anxiety by disrupting time for scholarly writing, the interpersonal element of such work and its effect on relationships with others was recognised as crucial. These findings highlight the centrality of writing relationships in academic identity and the role of digital technologies in both enabling and hindering them.

Our findings show how the changing conditions of academic life and workload affect the ways that academics are able to relate to others; not just to academic colleagues but also towards students and administrative and technical staff, on whom they rely heavily to produce successful writing. Some of these changes are experienced as beneficial while in other respects the overwhelming time demands lead people to try to minimise interruptions from others and to carve out a space where they can carry out the sustained thinking and writing they enjoy and see as essential to their complex roles.

Academics are engaged with different communities, including disciplinary and other professional networks that extend beyond their immediate employing institution. These can sometimes be at least as significant as people's immediate colleagues and managers, and loyalties may conflict as well as converge. This results in layers of internal and external relationships affecting academics' identity and shaping their writing work.

Our data reveal how practical wisdom about collaborative writing is informally developed. Such know-how is worth exploring in more detail. It includes knowledge of which technologies to use at different points in the writing process, the strategic use of face-to-face meetings between co-authors, use of time, negotiating power relationships and authorial leadership, how to sequence writing tasks and merge divergent voices. In the next chapter, we look more closely at the ways academics learn about writing together.

# 9

# LEARNING ACADEMIC WRITING

## An ongoing process

The previous chapters have described a picture of change in academics' writing practices through the ongoing introduction of new genres, demands, tools, and possibilities. Through this research we have found that the traditional model of training for an academic career – several years of focus on doctoral study, the production of a PhD thesis, and then perhaps a day or two of professional development events every year or so – does not provide the resources academics need to develop and understand the plethora of changing writing practices they have to contend with in their profession. As we have seen in previous chapters, the transformations occurring in the modern university require academics to constantly learn new practices. The demands of so-called "accountability writing" associated with managerialist approaches require the mastery of a range of new genres and new ways of representing oneself and one's work. Changes brought about by widespread digitisation in higher education have changed how academics collaborate and network with one another. As discussed in more detail in Chapter 6, file-sharing, video-conferencing, and other collaborative tools now provide new opportunities for working together. The internationalisation of higher education also affects many aspects of how and with whom academics collaborate. As pressure increases for research to have more international relevance and to be based on partnerships, there are a plethora of new skills and practicalities to be learned when collaborating with research colleagues and teams across time zones, spaces, languages, cultural practices, and networks (examined in more detail in Chapter 8).

In light of these transformations and challenges, we sought to examine how academics learn these new writing practices, and learn to adapt in a rapidly changing context. The previous chapter has shown the importance of relationships and collaborations in academics' writing lives. This chapter builds on that discussion to highlight the importance of informal, networked, and collaborative learning (see also McCulloch, Tusting, & Hamilton, 2017). We identify the significance of departmental culture and context in this learning process, and we explore some aspects of writing, such as email management, for which there is no shared learning process, and about which very little professional guidance is offered by institutions.

## Learning at the beginning of the career

The PhD is traditionally seen as being the main apprenticeship into academic life, training the scholar in independent research with the support of a supervisor after years of following a more structured taught educational route. It is a gatekeeping entry qualification, and a form of research training and experiential learning which is assumed to prepare an academic for university work (Green & Powell, 2005). In the techno-biographical interviews we carried out with participants, we asked them about the writing practices they had engaged with throughout their lives and careers, and how these related (or not) to their current working practices. During those interviews, PhD related writing was discussed, giving us an insight into the significance of this experience for learning to do what they do now.

It is clear that in terms of research writing, the process of doing a doctorate was indeed a formative experience for many of our participants, particularly in learning from the ongoing feedback from their supervisors. This was not just to do with the extent of the feedback, but also the type of feedback. Charles, for instance, from marketing, still retained clear memories of his experience of receiving informal feedback on an early chapter of his PhD:

> I remember when I did my PhD I was really chuffed with myself. "I've written that first complete chapter." It was part of the literature I was reading. I sent it to [my supervisor] who's one of the smartest guys I'll ever meet in my life, but he's also the loveliest guy you could ever meet ... I think he finds it very difficult to criticise, because he's such a nice guy. So I was trying to get some sort of constructive feedback. He's, "Mmm. It's a bit flowery". Then I read it and I was like, "Jesus Christ. It's like a Mills & Boon novel". He was like, "Just say what you say".

The feedback Charles received from the supervisor here was minimal and was carefully mitigated but, in the context of the positive supervisory relationship they had, this informal comment enabled him to reframe not just the chapter, but his whole approach to writing. Similarly, Larry, a multilingual academic whose first language was not English, received useful feedback from his PhD advisor on proofreading and improving his presentation, which provided him with confidence in writing academic texts.

Supervisors also played an important role in modelling approaches to writing. Lisa, an early career researcher in marketing, felt that:

> A lot of my writing practice has actually come from my supervisor, I'm learning through her. She was a big advocate of writing retreats and essentially trained me into that system, particularly post thesis ... when we've been working on papers together. I've learnt a lot from watching how she writes and mirroring that in some ways and finding out and realising that works for me in quite a big way.

Again, the personal connection with the supervisor is important. However, here, the learning is not about the crafting of sentences but about observing and imitating practices, in the manner of a traditional apprenticeship relationship.

Feedback from a PhD supervisor was not always such a positive or enjoyable learning process. Diane, now a senior, highly productive academic in marketing, also retained powerful memories of the influence of her supervisor's feedback, but these were much less constructive: "My PhD supervisor told me, 'You can't write. You can't write.' I was really upset and really worried." Diane's response to this was to turn to a friend who provided a different perspective.

> Then I had conversations with Dan who has been really important in my intellectual development. Dan thinks like me ... Dan said to me, "Writing is understanding". He said, "Start writing it because the writing is the knowing. It's not separate".

In her conceptualisation of her own writing development, the perspective received from a peer at the same stage, who she perceived to be similar to herself, was far more important and useful than the feedback from her supervisor. Where her supervisor's feedback stopped her from writing, the advice from her friend and colleague "freed me up to write". This positive learning relationship continued in the longer term, as Diane went on to co-author influential and well-received papers with Dan.

We saw from Diane, and others like her, that the process of learning to write associated with doing a doctorate did not happen only through formal aspects of the process such as supervisory feedback, but also through a number of informal aspects including learning from peers. But is this enough? For some time, it has been recognised that the doctoral process is an apprenticeship which prepares students for some aspects of professional academic life, particularly research, better than others (Green & Powell, 2005, pp. 50–52). In the context of the changes to the academic profession that we have discussed extensively already, we need to ask whether a doctorate provides adequate preparation for the changing demands which will be faced by new academic staff. If not, how do new academics keep pace with the many changes in their profession and their associated writing practices? As we will see below, processes of networked, informal, and collaborative learning are key to this.

### Learning from others: apprenticeship, collaboration, and networking

From our interviews, it is clear that the influence of informal connections and collaborations on the processes of learning to write in academia is significant. As participants continued to discuss how they had acquired and developed their writing practices through their careers, learning from others continued to be central. Writing for research purposes was learned through collaboration, through mentoring, and through receiving and reflecting on peer review, rather than primarily (or at all) through any kind of continued formal training. Mark, also in marketing but in the teaching-intensive university, describes his processes of learning academic writing as "an apprenticeship, rather than a formal sit in a classroom type thing". He said, "I haven't had any formal training. What I've done is work with people who are more intelligent and more capable than me, more experienced than me and worked with them and learned from them". Admittedly, Mark came from a successful career in business before entering academia, and consciously draws on the networking skills developed through that experience in developing his academic practices. But the importance of working with others to learn was also identified by our participants with a more exclusively academic background. Larry, the multilingual early career mathematician mentioned above, found putting together grant proposals a challenge. Submitting a proposal was a requirement of his probation, but he had had no formal training or experience in doing this. He consciously went about learning how to do this by getting feedback on early attempts from the lead of his research group, then from his head of department and his head of teaching, both very experienced professors who helped him to improve his presentation of the proposal.

Collaboration and learning from co-authors were key aspects of this learning, particularly where the co-authors were more experienced or had greater expertise in particular areas. Gareth, a mathematician, explained that "it's nice to be able to work with people who are more experienced, intellectually, down the line so they can guide the way. There's a guidance and a learning of what works". Colin, a historian, had mostly written as a sole author, as is typical in his field, but he found the few co-written articles he had worked on "fun to do" and said that he had "learnt a great deal from a super smart colleague". Both of these quotes illustrate a common pattern we saw in the data in which appreciation of what people had learned from more senior colleagues was combined with evaluative words like "nice" and "fun", signalling pleasure and enjoyment. As Charles told us, "The thing I really enjoy is when I send that paper off to another co-author and they say, 'That's great'. That's that point where you're learning". For this to work, however, it was important to find the right people to work with, as shown by Diane's discussion above of the difference between her supervisor's and her friend's input.

Learning from others was not always evaluated as a positive experience. Diane described her manager in an early academic post as having been someone whom she had learned from, but not in a positive way. "I worked with somebody there who was a micromanager. Yes, he made me a productive writer actually by being a bastard to be honest. It wasn't a pleasant experience but I learned a lot from it." Emma, an early career marketing academic, described a process of collaboration with more senior colleagues that seemed quite painful to her:

> I will write a paper. It will go to Tim. He will take it apart, tell me there's a million things that could be better. I will then rewrite it. It will then go back to Tim. It's still very much that I write the paper from end-to-end and then the collaborators take it and criticise it. Telling me that all my work is crap is certainly how it feels.

Although this kind of painful experience can lead to useful learning, it can also be counterproductive in terms of someone's developing identity as a writer. While Emma was happy that "when they do contribute it's brilliant", she found that the power relationships between herself as an early career researcher and these more senior academics kept her "very much in the student/supervisor dyad at this stage". In contrast, she had just begun to work on a special issue with two other women she had met at a conference who were at the same career stage as her and seemed to approach the area "from a similar point of view", and was enthusiastic and positive about this editing collaboration. Finding the right collaborators to work with and learn from, developing positive and sustaining personal networks, is clearly a key aspect of developing as an academic writer.

Learning from others did not always mean learning from other academics; other kinds of relationships could also be drawn on as learning resources. Kirsty, for instance, an administrator in a maths department, first started learned to use LaTeX from her husband, before getting some "pointers" from her boss and finally becoming a confident user by "picking it up along the way".

## Learning from others: peer review

Learning academic writing involves getting to grips with the conventions of quality, rigour, academic style, and fine-tuning an argument. The process of having journal articles peer-reviewed was mentioned by many as one of the key ongoing ways in which they were learning these kinds of conventions, particularly in relation to research writing. Emma, for instance, had sent a paper to three different, highly prestigious journals in her field, receiving peer-review feedback from two of them. While she had not yet been successful in getting the paper published, she felt that the feedback was very useful, particularly since it had come from the top journals in her area, and was helping her to learn what was necessary for successful publication in her field. Diane felt that her main difficulty with scholarly writing has been in finding ways to structure her ideas. She has learned to do this through learning from senior peers and colleagues (see the discussion of her relationship with Dan, above), but says that the main training she has had has come through the peer-review process: "occasionally you get really good reviewers on side who help you construct your argument. They don't change what you're trying to say, but they help you work out in which order to say it."

Peer review associated with edited collections, books, and special issues could similarly contribute to learning. Verity described an experience early in her career, when she was invited to contribute a chapter from her Master's dissertation to a book. Never having done such a thing before, "I literally took the spare copy, chopped it up, and sent it off, and got back a pained message saying, 'That won't do. Can you please actually write it properly?'" She described this as a learning curve in realising that she needed to actually rethink what she had written for her MA dissertation, rather than simply condensing it down to the appropriate word length.

## Learning from others: using models

One way of learning from others was, rather than speaking with or getting feedback from others, by drawing on others' writing as models. This seemed to be particularly important for genres such as grant proposals, which people would not necessarily have had extensive experience of either writing or reading. Bill, a mathematician in a research-intensive university, described his experience of learning to write grant applications as a combination of learning by doing and learning using models: "Give it a try. Get on with it. Here's a grant by a similar person. Have a look at that application and see what you can pick from it." Likewise, Nicola wanted to experiment with writing in an unconventional way for her first book, and found models to help her develop ways to do this.

> I would very much like to write it in a more engaging and creative style. That means unlearning and relearning new ways of writing. Fortunately, a lot of the historians I most admire have written for the publishers I'm interested in working with and have developed that style, so I'm learning how to do that through using those books as models.

Learning from models was not only important for academics but could also be crucial for learning administrative writing. Steve was a senior administrator at the large research-intensive university with key responsibilities for putting together REF submissions in particular. Despite the strategic importance of his work, he had had no specific training to prepare himself for his role. Rather, he described a process of picking it up as you go along, predominantly by looking at other documents: "You learn from things you like the look of. You see things and you think, 'I quite like that'", as well as learning from how the senior academics that he worked with regularly wrote documentation.

## Learning by doing

A particularly important aspect of learning was simply to learn by doing, by writing and reflecting on writing. Diane told us, "It's the practice of it. The more you do it, the better you get at it". She had acquired a particular discipline of writing through attending writing retreats:

> You do 90 minutes. When you've finished 90 minutes, even if you spend the last few minutes writing the next three bullet points, you do not get off your chair until you've finished the 90 minutes and then you have a break … That was an important part of my training, keep my bum on the seat.

Given everything we have discussed in previous chapters about the challenges of the competing priorities academics face, and the importance of setting boundaries around different kinds of writing tasks, learning ways to focus on particular kinds of writing work seems crucial. This can be as simple as learning what you want to say through the ongoing drafting and redrafting process. As Robert explains it,

> a lot of the time it's showing your stupidity, that as you go from version one to version two to version three, you're suddenly realising the thing you've said there wasn't at all the right way of saying that so you manipulate that a bit.

Like learning from collaboration, learning by doing could also be a deeply satisfying process. Charles spoke very positively about his experience of this process, saying, "It's that crafting. That learning of what we do and how to construct sentences, I enjoy that. When you feel that you've actually written something that makes sense". Patricia, a probationary marketing lecturer at a research-intensive university, talked about the pleasure she found in creating something new when organising her thoughts in writing, making notes on a topic and producing something visible on it:

> All aspects, all stages, in that kind of process are quite nice when I realise that I'm learning something new, I'm starting to understand this certain

topic and this literature and making sense of the different viewpoints, so that's always nice.

Having the opportunity to engage in writing regularly enough to learn by doing is not, however, evenly distributed. Mark, working in a teaching-intensive university with a heavy teaching load, pointed out:

> To be in four star, you need a big research budget to get that published. You need a lot of people to work with, you need a lot of time. But unless you get the time, you can't. So it's this chicken and egg situation whereby you can only get the hours if you've proven yourself to be able to get published, but you can only get published if you get the time and hours. So you go around in this circle.

## Learning to write for teaching

Most of the discussion above relates to research writing. However, the themes of learning from others, learning from feedback, and learning through experience also emerged when people discussed learning to write materials for teaching. Again, while some people had participated in teaching training programmes, most talked about an ongoing process of learning from feedback, from others, and from reflection on experience. Josh, an early career lecturer in a social sciences department, emphasised the importance of reflection, saying:

> I sit there and I look at what I've written and what I've put together and I try and put myself in the position of somebody that doesn't know the area. And it's trying to get that activity so self-explanatory on the sheets or on the handout or on the PowerPoint that I won't have like 20 or 30 different people asking me what the hell does it mean.

As he was relatively new to teaching, he felt that "it is very much at the moment learning as I'm going on. So I'm quite responsive to what the students are saying". Ella, an experienced marketing academic at the teaching-intensive institution, had learned all of her teaching-related writing practices through learning from others and learning by doing:

> Nobody has ever taught me to write lectures or to write revalidation documents. You just do it. You just get on and mimic what other people have been doing. I think then your own style grows out of that.

Mick, a marketing academic at the teaching-intensive university who had come from industry, was a very popular and successful teacher who had recently won a prestigious teaching award. He described using a range of innovative teaching methods, working intensively with students and using audio-visual methods for communication and feedback on students' work. He said that he had learned how to do this by "stand[ing] on the shoulders of giants", taking the best bits from all of his colleagues' teaching and putting them together in a package. He deliberately networked with as many people as he could, a practice he had brought from his previous business experience, "because networking in business is everything". Learning from others was at the heart of his approach to learning to teach, including learning how others approached teaching-related writing.

However, this predominance of informal learning in relation to teaching is changing, as early career lecturers are required to take teaching courses and gain higher education teaching qualifications. Bill, an experienced mathematician, reflected on how the landscape of higher education had changed in this regard. He, like many of his colleagues, had had his first experience of teaching when doing his PhD, which was very much a "learning by doing" experience: "the expectation was that you would do some teaching while you were doing your PhD and you would learn the ropes by doing and by seeing it done." His subsequent college teaching experience was similar: "I learnt to do that, basically, by getting the job, being given the students, and being told, 'It's your job to prepare them for these exams at the end of the year. Get on with it'." The situation has now changed. Many training courses in teaching are available, and he had recently in fact done an HEA-accredited training course. However, although this had led him to think more directly about teaching and learning activities, he still felt that "on the job is where I've really picked everything up, doing, observing and modifying".

## Learning writing for leadership and management

A lot of the administrative writing that people had to learn to do related to specific roles and responsibilities that they had in their department or institution. Even at the relatively senior level of head of department, most of the learning people talked about was still the kind of learning-by-doing we have seen in relation to the other spheres of academic work. Collin, head of a history department, felt that "I have to do this job for five years because the first three I've just been learning what I can't do and now I need to feel what I can do". Gareth, head of department in a maths department felt that "being Director [has] evolved through years of experience". Michael, in marketing at a large research-intensive institution, explained that being head of department was not difficult for him because he could draw on all the other big leadership roles in the department that he had carried out already, such as director of research: "I've done this, I've done that, I've been on all sorts of committees, I knew how the institution worked, I've seen colleagues in action, so in some respects it wasn't such a big deal with me."

Learning to manage people was one key aspect of adopting higher-level administrative roles which was described as being largely learned through experience. Annie, an early career researcher who had a principal investigator role on funded research projects, found that the training she had received on managing people, structured around long-term goals and interim reviews, was not well designed for managing research associates working on a short-term research project with rapidly evolving goals and tight deadlines. Instead, she developed a simple set of strategies supported by specific writing practices to keep the project on track, geared around a Friday afternoon summary of activities which she requested from her researchers, which then informed the agenda for a Monday morning planning meeting. She felt that this was a much more effective, simple set of writing practices than those she had been trained in; but the process of developing them was built on some rather difficult experiences that had damaged her confidence in herself as a manager.

Similar perspectives on training were held by most of our other participants, who tended to express the view that most of the formal training provided by their institution did not (and perhaps could not) directly address their learning needs. Generic management training, in particular, was seen to be a long way from what was needed in the academic sector. Michael, a head of department in marketing, told the story of a training session provided to incoming heads of department by a consultancy firm, in which the trainer began by congratulating the participants on their achievement at reaching the status of head. This, to him, showed the gulf between the assumptions made by the formal training organisation and the realities of a role which no one really wanted, and which was taken on as a service to the department rather than seen as an achievement.

The main value of formal training seemed to be in meeting others in the same role and being able to discuss shared issues – reinforcing the points made above about the importance of learning from others. Robert described a leadership programme he had attended, where he said:

> the useful thing about the leadership programme was not the programme itself, but some of the side things that they did ... the fascinating thing there was how everyone had problems and to realise that you weren't the only person who was having problems.

## Learning meta-logistical and organisational writing

When we broadened our lens and asked academics about *all* the types of writing that they did, we discovered many important, though often overlooked, writing tasks to do with self-organisation and control of work. Juliette, a senior academic in the social sciences, listed a complex interdependent set of texts and writing practices she used to organise her working day:

Post-Its, which I go through every day and I have a much longer-term to-do list thingy and then I have one for the day or for the week, so several to-do lists, which I need to keep on my mind. Then, I often have a couple of things I really want to get done that day as well, sometimes, they are actually just physically in my very old-fashioned paper diary, where I have meetings, but also in pencil, things that I really want to do, in between the official meetings and so on.

In contrast, Matt, the head of a maths department, adopted an entirely digital approach, using a calendar tool across devices for planning his time and a list management tool called Wunderlist to keep track of his to-dos. Each person we spoke to seemed to have their own strategy for organisational writing.

These are the kinds of writing to organise working life which Gornall and Salisbury (2012, p. 139) call the "meta-logistics of the modern academic workload", and Neumann (2009) calls the "work around the work": writing which is invisible to the organisation in terms of workload allocations but is a crucial part of the process of getting the work done. In contrast to some corporate settings where training in self-management, goal setting, and time management may be provided, it is rare for academics to have formal training in these kinds of tasks. In addition, in terms of self-organisation, it seems to be unusual for them to draw on the kinds of "learning from others" that we have identified as so important in relation to other roles and practices. Instead, the academics we spoke to seemed to each develop their own idiosyncratic practices, systems, and strategies for self-organisation through learning by doing, which changed as the demands in their working lives altered.

We have seen one example of this already in Chapter 6, when we discussed academics' experiences of email. It is clear that despite the fact that email has become the default mode of communication, there remains an enormous diversity in practices and attitudes around how academics can and should use it. Our earlier discussion made it clear that one of the major stressors in the lives of most of our participants was managing the flow of emails and their associated tasks. Given the ubiquity of email in academics' lives, its centrality as a means of communication, and the widely recognised difficulties it causes, one might imagine that here, at least, some kind of shared approach to email might be taught or at least codified by institutions. However, this was an area where formal training and learning from others were rarely mentioned. Only one academic in our data, Nicola, had received any training in this area, and this was in her previous role as an administrator. Expectations around dealing with email were therefore neither shared nor explicit, and this lack of shared learning to establish shared practices seemed to be one of the aspects of email which contributes to the common sense of being overwhelmed and lacking control.

## Learning social media and new technologies

As Chapter 7 has made clear, one area where practices are constantly changing is that of social media. We asked specifically about how people were learning to write on social media and whether they had undertaken any formal training in this. While there was a general consensus from our participants that attitudes towards social media have changed, and that online writing is now established as one of the legitimate writing practices academics might be expected to engage in, there was very little consensus as to how people had learned to do this or as to how this should be learned. This is partly because, as Mark from marketing points out, "the problem is that the people who generally drum up policies are pretty clueless on the whole world of social media. So I think they sort of left it to academic judgement". While some would welcome some input into this – Gareth, for instance, felt that "in terms of presenting yourself to the media, in some ways I think training is very valuable" – there was little agreement as to how this might best be done or even (as discussed in more depth in Chapter 7) as to what kind of engagement is most appropriate. While some people were waiting for clearer guidance from their departments and institutions, others quietly established their own social media practices. As Charles says, "it's something that's very much you just do what you want".

## Conclusion

Our work identifies many ways in which academics learn the writing practices of their work, most of which – learning from others; learning from feedback; learning from models; learning by doing – can be classed as relatively informal approaches to learning. Michael, a marketing academic, sums up the multiple ways in which people learn writing in this quote:

> By collaborating with people who had the craft, by talking to people who are successful, by trying my own things, by failing in quite a few others and by learning where to direct my energies, by looking at different styles of writing, different journals, different communities and so on. That was my training. There was nothing formal about it, it was very much like how you learn any other craft.

This is an aspect of academic life that some people very much appreciate. Robert, a mathematician, explained that "there's a continuous process of learning and finding out about new things, which I think is one of the really nice things of the job".

Learning through relationships and collaboration and from others' feedback was important in most of these areas, although less so in relation to personal administrative writing. One of the key themes to emerge in our data was the importance of nurturing positive and fruitful relations early in one's career, as part of the developing writing skills as an academic. This is not always so straightforward for many early career academics, and conversely, problems with writing and successfully publishing are often connected with problems of nurturing the right kind of networks in the field.

Our research has also highlighted the importance for our participants of adopting an autonomous, self-directed approach to learning writing. As Diane says, "To learn writing, you have to sort of sit there and do it yourself". Learning by doing was a central part of the picture of how academics learn writing, in all of the areas we looked at. One of the best ways to actually learn to write a particular genre, whether this be a new kind of paper, a grant proposal, or a new kind of administrative report, is to actually begin writing it and seek feedback on it as part of the process, linking learning by doing and the learning from others. However, this takes time and requires input from others which is not always easy to obtain. As Nicola explains,

> You have to have conferences, you have to teach, you have to do a zillion other things beyond the PhD to even stand a remote chance of getting a stepping stone onto a permanent job, so the majority of the skills that I learnt as a teacher and as an administrator and what not all took place long before I got to this point.

Considering the many changes that have occurred in academia through digitisation, corporatisation, and managerialism, among others (see Chapter 1), these learning strategies were very salient for our participants. What is striking is how individuated they are.

Where formal institutional training was mentioned, it was very frequently in relation to its weaknesses in preparing academics for their writing work. While people did talk about specific things learned from formal training – Josh, for instance, had learned not to overload his PowerPoint slides from a faculty training course – it was most likely to be positively evaluated where a training event had facilitated "learning by doing" or "learning from others". This raises some questions as to how academics can best be supported in their ongoing learning around writing, as the kinds of writing practices they engage in (and are expected to engage in) change and develop. It challenges us to think about how best to organise ongoing professional development, and highlights the importance of opening up opportunities for learning from one another and from more experienced colleagues, as well as for self-reflection. There are also implications for early career researchers. Returning to the question of how scholars are prepared for their work, it seems clear that the PhD itself, while a good preparation for working as an independent researcher, is not necessarily good training for the diversity of challenges associated with all the different types of writing academics engage in. Ultimately, it highlights the importance for individuals, departments, and institutions of opening up and maintaining opportunities for networking and collaboration. This is not always an easy thing to do in a pressured academic climate, but it is invaluable in terms of continued professional learning.

# 10

# THE FUTURES OF WRITING

## Conclusions and implications

This book has explored the nature of contemporary academic writing practices. We have asked how the current context in UK higher education affects writing practices, thereby shaping the nature of academic knowledge, and how this might change how we think about academic professional identity and the purposes of academia. In this final chapter, we reflect on our findings and identify their main points, returning to our initial aims and discussing themes that emerged from our data. We set out to look at writing and the dynamics of knowledge creation in the changing academy, addressing the overarching question of how knowledge is produced and distributed through the range of writing practices academics engage in, including scholarly, pedagogic, administrative, and impact writing. We looked for processes and explanations of how, where, when, with whom, and why academics write. We explored how academics' writing practices are shaped by socio-material aspects of the situation, including the affordances of physical spaces and other material resources; social relationships with peers, colleagues, students, and managers; and where they were located, in particular departments, universities, and disciplines. Because of the changing approaches to management associated with the corporatised university described in Chapter 1, we paid close attention to how managerial practices are shaping and co-ordinating academics' writing work. Given the importance of transformations in communication made possible by digital technologies, the role of such technologies in writing and knowledge creation was an essential part of the account.

In this chapter, we summarise our findings and then go on to discuss the implications of our research for individual academics, for departmental and institutional management, for training and professional development, and for higher education policy. We outline ways in which academic writing of all kinds can be supported, and ways of fostering positive writing cultures.

Finally, we lay out an agenda for research in this area, including examining how similar trends might be playing out internationally.

## Space and time

We have seen throughout the book how important it is to explore writing from a socio-material perspective. We have developed our approach to literacy practices accordingly, in order to attend to the spaces and times of writing and how people work within these. The background architecture of university campuses, communication technologies, and relationships constitute a changing infrastructure within which academic writing is accomplished.

The expansion of higher education as a global industry affects the physical environments in which people work and study day to day. The spaces of universities are designed with multiple purposes and users in mind, and the needs of academics' workplace writing are not usually at the forefront. Teaching spaces are enlarged to cater for bigger groups of students, libraries are reorganised as student friendly independent study and social spaces offering access to digital resources. Special attention is paid to the corporate public face of the university: signature buildings with prominent logos, open plan offices and smart reception areas displaying marketing information. In all three of the universities we studied, there was constant, disruptive building work going on as the physical estate was refurbished and extended.

The multiple roles and responsibilities of academic work lead to fragmented days and multiple interruptions, particularly when people are located in their university office. To manage this situation, our participants set boundaries around different types of writing, benefiting from the relative autonomy many academics still enjoy as to when and where they work. They produced different kinds of writing in different places. Most wrote at home, in cafés, and while travelling, as well as, or instead of, at their university workplace. They had different aesthetic and sensory needs and preferences in relation to writing spaces, and most of them found ways to spend at least some of their writing time in places which met these needs. They blocked out time for particular types of tasks, trying, where possible, to protect demanding writing tasks from interruptions and fragmentation.

However, it could be challenging to create boundaries of this kind. Despite the increased flexibility and opportunities that digital communication offers, the messages that flowed in on ever-present hand-held devices made it hard for people to stay free from interruptions in any given space. The different timescales associated with the multiple roles and responsibilities of academic professional life are hard to co-ordinate. Increasing workloads, and changes to the rhythms of the academic year, made it hard to find extended time to focus on research writing. To deal with the volume of work, many extended their writing across space and time. Boundaries between home and work spaces, and work and non-work times, often became blurred. The autonomy around when and where to work from which academics benefit, and which many of our participants appreciated, has therefore both positive and negative aspects.

## Managerialism

Throughout the book, we have discussed how the form, content, and quantity of academics' writing are shaped by managerialism; that is, influenced by institutional and departmental strategies put in place to manage academics' practices and performance. Many of the challenges described by the participants in our research relate to the introduction or development of increasingly managerialist approaches and the associated control technologies into the workings of their institutions, particularly in relation to accelerated through-put, strategic goal-setting, and accountability.

Managerial strategies at the senior level ultimately seek to safeguard and increase the financial security of institutions, through sustaining or increasing student recruitment and research funding income streams. Maintaining and improving a university's performance in national and international league tables is an important aspect of this. The ideology underlying such ranking systems is a belief in the value of re-constructing the higher education sector as a competitive marketplace, as well as a concern to ensure quantifiable transparency and accountability in the spending of public money.

The institutional strategies that have the most immediate effect on the writing practices of academics in their everyday working lives are usually those that aim to maintain and improve performance in a range of account-ability exercises which the league tables draw on. These included national evaluation exercises, particularly the REF, but also the National Student Survey (NSS). Quality assurance, appraisal, and promotion processes have also become increasingly explicitly informed by university-level strategies. Academics respond to such strategies and the associated managerial technol-ogies by making choices about and adapting their writing practices.

Teaching quality assurance processes and concerns to maximise NSS per-formance increased the volume of teaching and administration-related writing people were doing. Accountability requirements generated demands for representations of teaching activity in multiple formats and in new genres. Many of our participants felt that excessive time was spent producing listings and quantifiable representations of work, documenting the performance and outputs of individuals and academic units through form-filling and report writing. The audiences for such documents were often ambiguous or multiple, as were their purposes and consequences.

We found that all of the main areas of writing (research, teaching, admin-istration, and service) were influenced by managerialist strategies to some extent. The REF influenced many people's decisions about research writing, particularly in relation to the genre of publications and their location, prioritising journal articles in an often specific and limited range of highly rated journals. Such REF-driven priorities did not always reflect disciplinary perspectives on the types of writing that are most valuable and important. This led to tensions for some (though not all) of our participants between what is valued by institutional strategies, and what those individuals value in their writing.

The "techno-biographical" interviews we carried out provided insight into how such values were shaped by people's disciplinary training and personal histories. They showed how participants were driven by strong intrinsic and disciplinary motivations in their research work. The accountability mechanisms designed to encourage research writing productivity could be counterproductive, increasing people's anxiety rather than improving their writing. In addition, these strategies can have a more direct influence on the development of disciplinary knowledge. For instance, if people are publishing in journals that are chosen in relation to REF proxy measures, rather than in those which are read by their disciplinary communities, the networks of academic communication change. If people now publish short journal articles in preference to longer and more developed monographs, the nature of the arguments that can be developed is necessarily more constrained. REF-related pressures have the potential to deter some methodological approaches which require extended investment in time, such as for instance long-term ethnography. And some approaches to research are inherently riskier than others. If academics are pressed to produce a predictable number of outputs in a given time period, this can discourage the kind of research which pushes at the boundaries of existing knowledge without a guaranteed outcome.

## Digital technologies

Digital technologies are pervasive in academic life. They have changed how people access scholarly resources, opening up access to a huge and diverse range of research materials through university library systems and repositories, making it easier to access interdisciplinary perspectives on a given topic but much harder to claim scholarly mastery over a single field of research. They have changed how people communicate with students and colleagues; real-time collaboration is now possible with people all over the world. Teaching materials and feedback on work are increasingly located online, and teaching that was previously face-to-face is now often blended, with VLEs providing spaces for collecting lecture materials (and sometimes videos of lectures) as well as for online discussion and activities. Digital platforms are sold and maintained by large global corporations, beyond the control of individual universities. This can lead to challenges when interfaces change unexpectedly, or when new systems need to be learned at short notice.

Participants expressed a range of stances towards digital technologies. Some technologies, such as PowerPoint, generated neutral responses and were approached as tools, used in a range of different ways for different purposes by different participants. Others, such as email, elicited much more consistently negative responses. Email has become the default channel of communication amongst academics (but maybe not for students). Almost everyone accessed emails anywhere, using portable devices, particularly phones. Most people started the day by checking email, although some managed the constant influx of messages by setting boundaries, such as removing access to electronic devices at particular times of day. It was rare for academics to have received formal training around email, and departments had few clear expectations about email management practices.

One specific area where digitisation has led to rapid transformation is in the area of social media, where academics now have many more possibilities available to them for publicising their work and constructing an online identity. This generated diverse responses from our participants. While social media represented opportunities for engaging with wider audiences, particularly important given the additional focus on impact which is part of the REF pressure mentioned above, it is also associated with risks. These include the risks which come with a higher level of public exposure, as well as risks of increased workload online or distraction away from more highly valued types of writing. Some of our participants were in a position to be able to reject engagement with social media entirely, but others – particularly those in more precarious positions, such as those on probation – showed evidence of having thought through their social media engagement more strategically. The institutional and individual consequences of academics engaging with social media are likely to become more complex, especially in the light of concerns about personal data marketing and surveillance.

## Relationships, collaboration, and informal learning

Our study has highlighted the importance of understanding academics' writing not as individual practices, but as always part of broader relationships and collaborations, whether in relation to research writing, teaching, administration, or service. Collaboration between colleagues within and across institutions was an important aspect of most people's writing lives, particularly in relation to research writing, challenging the underlying model of evaluation of universities through competitive rankings systems. Digital technologies sometimes enabled collaborative writing relationships, and sometimes hindered them; digital communication alone was rarely felt to be enough to build and sustain productive collaborative writing relationships. People needed to meet face-to-face, especially in the early stages of collaboration. Many of our participants had developed substantial practical wisdom about how to combine different communication technologies and strategies to achieve successful collaboration. Divisions of labour between academics and administrative staff have also changed over time, and while there was variation across sites, digital platforms for research, teaching and administration across universities compel academics and professional services staff to work interdependently.

Change was a constant theme in our data, and, therefore, learning to deal with and respond to such change is important. Relationships with colleagues were particularly important in learning new academic writing practices. Our findings highlight the many genres of writing academics need to master, and their rapidly changing nature. As aspects of the workplace context change, new roles and genres are introduced. People have to continually re-learn how to be an academic, and how to engage in new writing tasks. Ongoing informal learning in the workplace, mainly from other people, but also from adapting models of particular genres, was key to coping with this situation of constant change, not just at the start of people's academic careers but throughout their working lives. The importance of such informal learning can be contrasted with formal training, which was frequently described as being somewhat removed from the realities of people's working and writing lives and was also difficult to access in the already overcrowded timetable of the working day.

## Stress and pressure

One theme that runs throughout our data is the high level of stress and pressure described by many participants (and also by those we invited to participate, but who were not able to commit to yet another demand on their time). This is consistent with other research which shows high and increasing levels of stress, excessive workloads, and poor work–life balance in UK higher education (e.g. UCU, 2015; Taberner, 2018). These tensions are exacerbated by the intensification of work and job flexibility/insecurity (see Barberis, 2013).

Given the amount of stress which was reported, it is surprising that there were very few examples of overt resistance to working and writing conditions in our data, and no real evidence of collective resistance until the strike action with which we opened this book, which took place after our data had been collected. One or two of our participants described resisting some demands, like Dolly's rejection of administrative demands that were felt to be unreasonable. Most seemed rather to continually try to find ways to manage the tasks that were being asked of them by their departments and institutions, alongside the other projects they had personally committed to. Despite the prevalence of experiences of stress and overload across our data set, there seemed to be a tendency for people to individualise their experiences, saying things like "I'm really rubbish with email", for instance, rather than "I receive more emails than it is possible to cope with in this amount of time".

James Scott suggests that such expressions of stress and tension in everyday life can be seen as symptoms of resistance that may build over time, eventually erupting as violent interactions, anger or collective mobilisation:

the necessity of "acting a mask" in the presence of power produces, almost by the strain engendered by its inauthenticity, a countervailing pressure that cannot be contained indefinitely.

*(Scott, 1990, p. 9)*

Thus, everyday, mundane acts and "workarounds" which may be primarily symbolic or language-related can appear to be insignificant, but a growing body of international literature shows it is important to document these in order to understand the genesis and dynamics of collective, organised movements and resistant events (Johansson & Vinthagen, 2016).

Stress and pressure do not always have negative effects While pressure associated with the REF, for instance, can cause anxiety, it can also encourage people to produce the kinds of publications that will enable their work to have a wider impact and contribute to their own career progression and promotion. Being faced with more demands than seem to be possible to complete in the time available can generate creative approaches to time management and mastery of new practices. But there is a balance to be struck here, and our work reinforces the suggestion that at the moment the balance is tipped a little too far in the wrong direction within the accelerated academy (Carrigan, 2015b).

This tension is a logical consequence of the corporatisation and commodification of the university. If higher education is to become a sector which works within the logic of the competitive market, it makes sense to try to get as much output from staff for as little outlay as possible. We see the effects of this, for instance, in people's individualisation and internalisation of the demands of the REF. This is reinforced by a culture of over-achievement and the commitments of many academics to their work as a vocation, rather than just a job.

We have demonstrated in this book the concrete effects of such systemic changes in the higher education sector at the level of individuals' workplace experiences. This plays out on many fronts, including influencing the kind of research which people are carrying out, shaping the kinds of teaching people are able to do, and minimising risk-taking in many areas of higher education. Having said that, we have also seen how people identified characteristics of their working and writing lives that gave them great pleasure and satisfaction; but many of these had both positive and negative aspects. For instance, people appreciated the freedom and the autonomy they had to arrange their own working lives and to be able to work from home. On the down side, this was also what made it possible for email conversations to continue into the early hours. People enjoyed having the freedom to develop their own research agendas and plan their research writing around that; but in the context of the accountability systems and strategies that we have been discussing, this very freedom can lead to over-commitment and hyper-performativity which can be counterproductive to creative thinking and risk-taking. While some individuals may benefit from the rewards available to the hyper-performing, we need to ask whether this is overall a positive aspect of higher education, or whether the associated costs in terms of workplace stress, employment equality, or the capacity to take the risks to pursue genuinely new (and hence uncharted, un-timeable, and unpredictable) forms of knowledge, are really too high.

This issue plays out not only in relation to individuals' motivations for writing, which can be conflicted, but also relates to the broader issue of the perceived purposes of universities. If universities are predominantly to be spaces to produce skilled graduates to service the national economy, then perhaps this is not so serious. But if we feel that there is an intrinsic benefit to having a space in society for constructive social critique and creative thinking and research, such activities become more difficult under the conditions that this research has described.

## Knowledge creation and different visions of writing identities

We have identified in this study the wide diversity of ways in which academics create knowledge. The work of writing journal articles and monographs is to report research findings. Teaching materials, course handbooks, and feedback to students create knowledge for learning. Social media engagement produces representations of research knowledge and of academic identity. Administrative knowledge is produced in reports to faculty or minutes of committee meetings. Knowledge for one's own use about work commitments and plans is manifested in the production of to-do lists and task outlines. Some of these genres are well established, while others are new and still relatively unformed. Academics' writing is multi-layered, and many of these layers are invisible and never become public.

This creation of knowledge by academics is shaped by many factors: personal history; disciplinary allegiance and values; departmental and institutional strategies; relationships and collaborations. Every day, academics have to choose, amongst the many different writing tasks they are committed to, which ones they will actually do; and every day, there are too many to contemplate doing all of them. Factors people bear in mind in making these choices include local and material issues of time and resources available, urgency, and perceived importance. But broader factors also come into play, with people balancing their allegiances: to their own personal career paths or to institutional strategies; to local colleagues or to research collaborators in other institutions and disciplinary communities; to students or to research participants. Choosing one writing task is always to let all of the other writing go, and hence to neglect these other allegiances and commitments, at least for a while. Digital forms of communication are enabling new groups to form – Facebook groups, WhatsApp connections, online writing groups – with their own potential for offering support, but also their own sets of demands. Every time a writing task is embarked upon, new conflicts between identities, allegiances, and commitments can arise.

People often expressed pleasure and high motivation for the research-related writing they engaged in, and indeed for teaching-related writing such as producing teaching materials. They were much more ambivalent about administrative-related writing, distinguishing it from the "real" writing and complaining that imposed administrative writing tasks were taking away time needed to get this "real" writing done. This could be because administrative writing is experienced as boring, imposed rather than self-generated, and it may be related to procedures that are not seen to be useful or productive. However, there may be a deeper reason for this feeling that such writing is not "real", which is to do with different ideologies or visions of what writing is, and how writing relates to people's identities as academics.

There is a traditional vision of "academic writing" that is central to academic work and for which academics have been trained and socialised: it is writing that relates to research and the diffusion of disciplinary knowledge and ideas, often dealing with new knowledge or knowledge significantly related to the author's core commitments and interests, even where this is produced through collaborations among scholars. Administrative writing is very different from this vision. However, writing administrative documents like reports, reviews, and action plans could also be termed "academic writing", in the sense that they underpin much of the work that goes on in higher education. This kind of writing is action-oriented. It deals with practical procedures, rules, and policy strategies. It can draw on important underlying philosophies of knowledge and action. It can be highly innovative (and creative) in the realities it is designed to bring about. But it has a radically different vision of authorship, audience, and purpose from the traditional view described above.

Authorship of an administrative text is dispersed, and not necessarily always across authors who share the same point of view on the text. In fact, conflicting viewpoints and values and different levels of expertise and commitment to the text are the norm. The text is not owned by any individual but is the property of the institution (at some level). Audiences are multiple and shifting and may not even engage with the text once it is written, since the text exists to enact decisions or to show legal compliance. The text, once written, is not fixed, but can be taken up and changed beyond recognition by further groups of writers and repurposed for new audiences. However, it is a powerful form of writing and can be a source of considerable creative satisfaction.

Perhaps academics' resistance to this kind of writing is to do with orienting to a different vision of what writing and being a writer is, that conflicts with the perspective and approach needed to engage productively with writing for administrative purposes. If so, the converse is that people socialised and trained in administrative functions may find it hard to understand the frustrations academics express about administrative writing. When this conflict is overlaid with threats to academic identity from managerialism and changing technologies, unwillingness to engage with administrative functions is even more understandable.

## Implications: fostering a positive writing culture in academia

We have developed our understanding of how current pressures and systems are affecting the construction of academic knowledge through shaping writing practices and considered the effects of this for academics' working and writing practices and identities. This work has implications for individual academics and professional services staff; for management at the level of the department and the institution; for training and professional development; and for policy makers. When we fed back our initial analyses at impact events, people asked two different kinds of questions. The first were about how we could advise them in terms of managing their writing successfully within the pressures of the current system. The second were about how we could contribute to changing the system. In the discussion that follows, both of these aspects will be considered.

### Implications for academics

The first implication that we would draw out for individual academics is simply to underline the commonalities amongst the patterns identified above. We would encourage people to understand difficulties they may have with writing from a systemic perspective, rather than engaging in the kind of individual self-blame that we have often seen, particularly when these relate to management of workload and especially in managing the influx of email. Likewise, writing success should not be seen solely as the achievement of an individual, as it depends on support from other people, time, and access to institutional resources. Recognition that writing issues are shared across disciplines and across different universities, and discussion of how we might want academic writing to be organised, are the first steps towards organising a more supportive writing environment.

As a more immediate response to the stresses and pressures identified above, we have written about the strategies people developed to manage the multiple writing demands they faced. We have identified the importance of constructing boundaries to create protected time and space for working on specific types of highly valued writing, away from interruptions; and we have written about the importance of relationships and collaboration with others in many aspects of people's writing lives.

While we have mainly written about the creation of boundaries at the level of the individual, increasingly, the construction of protected writing spaces and times in community with others is becoming a recognised vernacular practice in academia. In recent years, writing in community, either face-to-face or online, in writing groups or writing retreats, has become a much more common practice. This provides both a structure for protected writing time and support from others focusing on the same activity.

In part, this movement has spread through social media. "Shut up and Write Tuesdays" (@SUWTues), a Twitter feed that co-ordinates academics to write together for set periods of time in a focused way once a week, started in 2013, inspired by the Shut Up and Write movement of fiction writers which started in San Francisco in 2007. The original feed, hosted in Australia, has nearly 5,000 followers, and the UK (@SUWTUK) and North American (@SUWTNA) timezone feeds have nearly 3,000 apiece. Face-to-face academic writing retreats have also become a more common aspect of academic life, with Rowena Murray a pioneer in this field in the UK. Mentioned by some of our participants, her retreats provide focused writing time slots and a structured approach using writing prompts. This is based on years of experience and research (Murray & Newton, 2009). But she is not alone: as the concept of academic writing in community has become more familiar (Antoniou & Moriarty, 2008), people across many universities are setting up their own protected spaces for this. This can be as simple as booking a room for a few people for a morning on a regular basis and committing to writing during that time. Our work in this book supports the creation of such boundaried spaces and times, alone and with others, as a way to create positive opportunities for writing (and, as discussed above, not only research-related writing) in academics' working lives.

## Implications for management

Individuals and groups cannot create positive writing cultures if the system they are working in is set up in ways which are inimical to this. Our findings also have implications for those in positions of management responsibility in universities, both at the level of the department and at more senior levels.

At the departmental or equivalent level, heads of department play an important, though often challenging, role in mediating between the requirements of central strategies and procedures and the day-to-day working lives of staff. Heads and departmental management teams can explicitly set expectations around working spaces, email practices, and the balance between teaching, administration, and research responsibilities in ways which recognise the need for protected writing time for some kinds of writing and which respect academics' autonomy to organise their own spaces and times for different kinds of work. We found examples in our data where this was being done and was appreciated.

In relation to email in particular, open discussions in departments to agree shared expectations about the kinds of issues that should and should not be addressed in email and particularly about what is a reasonable response time can address the issue of unspoken expectations about email pressures and begin to co-develop practices around how to use email that support, rather than sabotage, the other aspects of academics' work. Heads of department also need to bear in mind that writing for administrative purposes involves engagement with another demanding set of genres which take time and creative energy to prepare. They need to understand the potential real impact that doing a lot of administrative writing can have on the time and energy people have for other kinds of writing.

At the higher level of central university management, managers must seriously think about, and monitor unintended consequences of, centralised approaches to the encouragement of particular types of academic writing for strategic institutional purposes. The goal of REF-related strategies is to boost the production of research which will be rated as internationally or world-leading; but constraining people to publish in particular ways and in particular locations may well work against production of the kind of innovative, creative work which the notion of "world-leading research" implies. Generally speaking, academics are ambitious over-achievers. They need support, rather than performance management, to enable them to produce the best research writing they can.

Management should also recognise where people are being placed in double-binds; where research writing is perceived as being the most important thing for promotions purposes, but where people are so stretched by the responsibilities of teaching and administration that the only time they can do their research writing is outside usual working hours. Several of our participants talked about this as the normal, expected state of working life in academia; but it is not normal or healthy that promotion and progression should depend on extending working hours in this way.

This is an issue which has serious equality implications for the sector, particularly in relation to people who have caring responsibilities which make the extension of writing work over time and space difficult or impossible. We know that women still take on a disproportionate level of caring responsibilities, for children and for other dependents (Misra, Lundquist, & Templer, 2012; Probert, 2005), and we know that there is a problem with the gender pay gap in academia, particularly at higher grades. In 2018, a government data collection exercise on pay and gender showed women in higher education earning 16.5% less than men by median average, in comparison to a median gender pay gap across all employers of only 9.7% (Pells, 2018). This is an issue that university management across the sector have an urgent duty to address.

### Implications for workplace learning and professional development

This research has highlighted the importance of informal learning in communities and through professional relationships, in order for academics to learn the multiple writing practices in which they are engaging. This does not mean there is no role for organised workplace learning or professional development. It does, though, imply that one of the most important things dedicated training sessions can provide is the opportunity for academics to learn from one another, recognising what people already know and drawing out the implicit practical knowledge (for instance, about how they deal with digital technologies, or how they go about collaborative writing) that they may take for granted. The specificities and complexities of the academic writing context also imply that bringing in consultants and trainers from other industries is likely to be limited in its impact. The work also highlights the value, when passing on administrative roles and responsibilities, of having a shadowing period where the incoming person can learn from the outgoing one, and of sharing models of documents in genres which are new to people to provide examples to work from.

Our findings have particular significance for those involved in supporting and training early career researchers (as evidenced by the multiple invitations our project has already received from research development staff). Reflection on setting boundaries, spaces and times of writing, managing multiple tasks and genres, using electronic devices, email management, choices around social media engagement, and making expectations clear would all be useful for people starting out in an academic role, as well as explicit discussion of how the PhD writing process can be quite different from the process of writing for publication while managing other academic responsibilities. Such discussions could also be built into research student training programmes.

## Future research

### *Extending the study*

This study was, as all studies are, constrained by its own particularities. By focusing in depth, using repeated interviews and observations, on the experiences of a relatively small number of academics, disciplines, and institutions, we were able to generate and test good understandings of a wide range of characteristics of their writing practices. The arguments we have presented in this book resonate with our own experience, and when we have presented this work at impact events and at conferences, it clearly rang true for the audiences too. The impact events in particular helped us to understand how important it is to articulate the writing experiences of academics in this detailed way, as our audiences responded with recognition and support to our findings and pushed us to develop their implications further.

In-depth qualitative work of this kind can always be built on and developed more broadly. Further research on academics' writing could expand beyond the specific sites we studied. We focused in on three disciplines, and we have seen how each of these had their own unique features and responses to the contemporary context. Extending the work to include people working in other disciplines would develop the perspectives further. It would be interesting, for instance, to do similar work in lab-based scientific disciplines, where individuals' research writing may be produced as part of a much larger group.

Future work could also extend the comparison we began here between different types of institutions. Some of the differences between the teaching-intensive institution we worked in and the two research-intensive institutions, such as frequency of restructuring, different degrees of prioritisation of teaching, and different expectations about and resources allocated to research writing, may well be common across other institutions. Having said that, another thing that was underlined for us in doing this work was the messiness among and across the divisions of discipline and institution with which we began. Subsequent work would need to be prepared for the fact that the neat theoretical divisions rarely hold in practice.

Finally, this work could be extended to other fields where writing is a key part of the work; other professions such as medicine or law, or knowledge-driven industries like software design. We would expect to see similar patterns particularly where centralised accountability systems and a competitive approach have been introduced to a field which was previously characterised by more professional autonomy, and where people are responding to frequent and rapid change.

## *Methodology*

Some of our experiences in carrying out the data collection can usefully inform future work in this area. As we were recruiting participants, particularly for the core phases 1 and 2 of the research, we saw clear patterns in the responses of who was willing to work with us. It was noticeably harder to recruit women, people in precarious employment situations, and people whose first language was not English. As a result these groups are under-represented among our core partici-pants, though we did make a special effort to redress this balance in our phase 3 data. Other work in this area has reported similar patterns, see for example Taberner (2018). As mentioned earlier, we feel this reflects some of the broader structural inequalities which still exist in higher education; these are groups who are already under pressure and thus find it harder to agree to engage in addi-tional activities. Future research could focus specifically on these groups, but careful thought would need to be given to designing an approach which is rea-listic in its expectations of time and commitment, perhaps by carefully planning data collection with participants for quieter times of the year.

People who did participate in the research often expressed pleasure and satisfaction in the process. Several of them have fed back to us that they found value in having talked explicitly about these issues during their inter-views, and that the provision of such a space for reflection on writing seemed to prove useful for them. However, we also learned where people's sensitivities lay. The stage 2 screen-in-screen recording process, in particular, required careful negotiation, and several of our participants were not happy to be involved with this. The fact that academics engage in writing in many places also meant that it was harder to observe the writing process than we had expected. For ethical reasons and because the recording technology had to be set up in people's offices, our observations were limited and sometimes artifi-cially set up.

## International academics writing

One obvious way to extend this research is to explore similar issues in different international contexts. Academia is a globally interconnected network of institutions, academics, and research projects all involved in the work of knowledge production. The kinds of systems and structures we have discussed in relation to the UK system here in this book are being introduced around the world, and with research productivity now linked closely with internationalisation, many academics face particular challenges due to their locations. Academics in the Global South and in emerging economies face particular resource constraints and infrastructural problems that render their experience very unequal when attempting to collaborate with partners based in elite universities.

Added to this, with globally accepted rankings criteria as a universal measurement of quality, and English as the official language of most science and academic publishing, there is a kind of convergence that promotes a unity of vision for how a university is managed, its function and aims, as well as how academics do their job and produce knowledge for an international audience. With Asian universities, particularly those within China, now producing more scientific outputs than universities in the United States and Europe (Johnson, Watkinson, & Mabe, 2018), the concerns raised within this book are therefore likely to arise for academics in other countries, exacerbated by the dominance of English in global academic publishing and pressures to publish in English (Lillis & Curry, 2010).

## Conclusion

The weight of evidence we collected and the feedback we have received about our findings suggest a level of discomfort among academics with the current conditions under which they carry out their writing work. In writing this book we have followed a fine line. On the one hand we acknowledge this discomfort, unpicking the reasons for it (including the pressures arising from the marketisation and digitisation of higher education) and suggesting strategies for change. On the other hand, we recognise that for many people, becoming an academic is still a desired profession, which offers the opportunity to pursue creative and socially valuable work, centred around writing and productive collaborations, with the flexibility to organise daily activities to a greater extent than many other jobs. These positive experiences are not distributed equitably, and writing is experienced differently in different universities and at different career stages. Where access to resources is limited, tensions are highlighted and this seems to be particularly the case in relation to the precious resources of time for chosen writing. However, we do see reasons for hope: in the self-organisation of communal writing support; in the growing recognition of the issues we identify as issues of importance for the sector as a whole; and in the moments of more organised resistance such as those with which we began this book. After all, the practices of academic writing are the central processes by means of which we produce, extend, develop, and transmit knowledge. Finding ways to organise universities as workplaces which support these practices is of the highest priority.

# REFERENCES

Adam, B. (2008). The timescapes challenge: Engagement with the invisible temporal. Paper presented at the Timescapes (ESRC Longitudinal Study). Leeds: University of Leeds. Retrieved from www.cardiff.ac.uk/socsi/resources/Leeds%20talk%20prose %20Timescapes%20Challenge%20250208.pdf

Ainsworth, S., Grant, D., & Iedema, R. (2009). "Keeping things moving": Space and the construction of middle management identity in a post-NPM organization. *Discourse & Communication*, 3(1), 5–25.

Antoniou, M., & Moriarty, J. (2008). What can academic writers learn from creative writers? Developing guidance and support for lecturers in higher education. *Teaching in Higher Education*, 13(2), 157–167. doi:10.1080/13562510801923229

Barberis, P. (2013). The managerial imperative: Fifty years' change in UK public administration. *Public Policy and Administration*, 28(4), 327–345.

Barnett, R. (2000). University knowledge in an age of supercomplexity. *Higher Education*, 40(4), 409–422.

Baron, N. S. (1998). Letters by phone or speech by other means: The linguistics of email. *Language & Communication*, 18(2), 133–170. doi:10.1016/S0271-5309(98)00005-6

Barton, D. (2007). *Literacy: An introduction to the ecology of written language* (Second edition). Oxford: Blackwell.

Barton, D., & Hamilton, M. (2000). Literacy practices. In D. Barton, M. Hamilton, & R. Ivanič (Eds.), *Situated literacies: reading and writing in context* (pp. 7–15). London and New York: Routledge.

Barton, D., & Hamilton, M. (2012). *Local literacies: Reading and writing in one community* (Second edition). London: Routledge, 1998.

Barton, D., Hamilton, M., & Ivanič, R. (Eds.) (2000). *Situated literacies: Reading and writing in context*. London: Routledge.

Barton, D., & Lee, C. (2013). *Language online: Investigating digital texts and practices*. Abingdon: Routledge.

Barton, D., & Papen, U. (Eds.) (2010). *The anthropology of writing*. London: Continuum.

Barton, D., & Tusting, K. (Eds.) (2005). *Beyond communities of practice: Language, power and social context.* Cambridge: Cambridge University Press.

Baynham, M., & Prinsloo, M. (Eds.) (2009). *The future of literacy studies.* Basingstoke: Palgrave Macmillan.

Bazerman, C. (1997). The life of genre, the life in the classroom. In W. Bishop & H. Ostrom (Eds.), *Genre and writing issues, arguments, alternatives* (pp. 19–26). Portsmouth, NH: Boynton.

Bazerman, C. (2005). A response to Anthony Fleury's "Liberal education and communication against the disciplines": A view from the world of writing. *Communication Education,* 54(1), 86–91.

Becher, T., & Trowler, P. R. (2001). *Academic tribes and territories.* Milton Keynes: Society for Research in Higher Education/Open University Press.

Bellotti, V., Ducheneaut, N., Howard, M., Smith, I., & Grinter, R. (2005). Quality versus quantity: E-mail-centric task management and its relation with overload. *Human-Computer Interaction,* 20(1), 89–138.

Bennett, L., & Folley, S. (2014). A tale of two doctoral students: Social media and hybridised identities. *Research in Learning Technology,* 22. doi:10.3402/rlt.v22.23791

Bhatia, V. K. (1993). *Analyzing genre: Language use in professional settings.* London: Longman.

Bhatt, I. (2017a). *Assignments as controversies: Digital literacy and writing in classroom practice.* New York: Routledge.

Bhatt, I. (2017b). Classroom digital literacies as interactional accomplishments. In M. Knobel & C. Lankshear (Eds.), *Researching new literacies: Design, theory, and data in sociocultural investigation* (pp. 127–149). New York: Peter Lang.

Blommaert, J. (2013). *Ethnography, superdiversity and linguistic landscapes: Chronicles of complexity (critical language and literacy studies).* Clevedon: Multilingual Matters.

Borgman, C. L. (2007). *Scholarship in the digital age.* Cambridge, MA: The MIT Press.

Bowker, G. C., & Star, S. (2000). *Sorting things out: Classification and its consequences.* Cambridge, MA: The MIT Press.

Brandt, D. (1998). Sponsors of literacy. *College Composition and Communication,* 49 (2), 165–185.

Brandt, D., & Clinton, K. (2002). Limits of the local: Expanding perspectives on literacy as a social practice. *Journal of Literacy Research,* 34(3), 337–356. doi:10.1207/ s15548430jlr3403_4

Burawoy, M. (2005). For public sociology. *American Sociological Review,* 70, 4–28.

Callon, M. (2002). Writing and (re)writing devices as tools for managing complexity. In J. Law & A. Mol (Eds.), *Complexities: Social studies of knowledge practices* (pp. 191–218). Durham, NC: Duke University Press.

Cardenas, M. L., & Rainey, I. (2018). Publishing from the ELT periphery: The Profile journal experience in Columbia. In M. L. Curry, & T. Lillis (Eds.), *Global academic publishing: Policies, perspectives and pedagogies* (pp. 151–165). Blue Ridge Summit: Multilingual Matters.

Carrigan, M. (2015a, July 21). The cognitive costs of escaping the filter bubble. Retrieved from http://markcarrigan.net/2015/07/21/the-cognitive-costs-of-escaping-the-filter-bubble/

Carrigan, M. (2015b, April 7) Life in the accelerated academy: Anxiety thrives, demands intensify and metrics hold the tangled web together. In *LSE Impact of the Social Sciences Blog.* Retrieved from http://blogs.lse.ac.uk/impactofsocialsciences/ 2015/04/07/life-in-the-accelerated-academy-carrigan/

Castells, M. (2010). *The rise of the network society: The information age: economy, society, and culture* (Vol. 1) (Second edition). Oxford: Wiley-Blackwell.

Chang, H. (2008). *Autoethnography as Method*. Walnut Creek, CA: Left Coast Press, Inc.

Chubb, J., Watermeyer, R., & Wakeling, P. (2017). Fear and loathing in the academy? The role of emotion in response to an impact agenda in the UK and Australia. *Higher Education Research and Development*, 36(3), 555–568. https://doi.org/10.1080/07294360.2017.1288709

Corrall, S., & Keates, J. (2011). The subject librarian and the virtual learning environment: A study of UK universities. *Program: Electronic Library and Information Systems*, 45(1), 29–49.

Cortez, M. (2013, September 28). The dangers of academic blogging. Retrieved from http://tirnscholars.org/2013/10/03/the-dangers-of-academic-blogging-via-sociologica l-imagination-blog/

Dale, K., & Burrell, G. (2007). *The spaces of organisation & the organisation of space: Power, identity & materiality at work*. New York: Palgrave.

Deem, R., Hillyard, S., & Reed, M. (2007). *Knowledge, higher education, and the new managerialism: The changing management of UK universities*. Oxford: Oxford University Press.

Denis, J., & Pontille, D. (2015). Material ordering and the care of things. *Science, Technology, & Human Values*, 40(3), 338–367.

Felt, U., Igelsböck, J., Schikowitz, A., & Völker, T. (2016). Transdisciplinary sustainability research in practice: Between imaginaries of collective experimentation and entrenched academic value orders. *Science, Technology, & Human Values*, 41(4), 732–761. doi:10.1177/0162243915626989

Fenwick, T., & Edwards, R. (2014). Networks of knowledge, matters of learning, and criticality in higher education. *Higher Education*, 67, 35–50. doi:10.1007/s10734-10013-9639-9633

Fenwick, T., & Nerland, M. (2014). *Reconceptualising professional learning: Sociomaterial knowledges, practices and responsibilities*. Abingdon and New York: Routledge.

Fenwick, T., Nerland, M., & Jensen, K. (2012). Sociomaterial approaches to conceptualizing professional learning and practice. *Journal of Education and Work*, 22(1), 1–13.

Fisher, D., Brush, A. J., Gleave, E., & Smith, M. A. (2006). Revisiting Whittaker & Sidner's "e-mail overload" ten years later. Proceedings of the 2006 20th Anniversary Conference on Computer Supported Cooperative Work – CSCW '06.

Fraiberg, S. (2010). Composition 2.0: Toward a multilingual and multimodal framework. *College Composition and Communication*, 62(1), 100–126.

Garcia, C. M., Eisenberg, M. E., Frerich, E. A., Lechner, K. E., & Lust, K. (2012). Conducting go-along interviews to understand context and promote health. *Qualitative Health Research*, 22(10), 1395–1403.

Goodfellow, R. (2013). The literacies of "digital scholarship": Truth and use values. In R. Goodfellow & M. Lea (Eds.), *Literacy in the digital university: Critical perspectives on learning, scholarship, and technology* (pp. 67–78). London: Routledge.

Goodfellow, R., & Lea, M. R. (2013). *Literacy in the digital university: Critical perspectives on learning, scholarship and technology*. London: Routledge.

Gornall, L., Cook, C., Daunton, L., Salisbury, J., & Thomas, B. (2013). *Academic working lives: Experience, practice and change*. London: Bloomsbury.

Gornall, L., & Salisbury, J. (2012). Compulsive working, "hyperprofessionality" and the unseen pleasures of academic work. *Higher Education Quarterly*, 66(2), 135–154. doi:10.1111/j.1468-2273.2012.00512.x

Gourlay, L. (2012). Media systems, multimodality and posthumanism: Implications for the dissertation? In R. Andrews, E. Borg, S. Boyd-Davis, M. Domingo, & J. England (Eds.), *SAGE handbook of digital dissertations and theses* (pp. 85–100). Thousand Oaks: Sage.

Gourlay, L. (2014). Creating time: Students, technologies and temporal practices in higher education. *E-Learning and Digital Media*, 11(2), 141–153.

Green, H., & Powell, S. (2005). *Doctoral study in contemporary higher education*. Maidenhead: SRHE and Open University Press (McGraw-Hill Education).

Greenhow, C., & Gleason, B. (2014). Social scholarship: Reconsidering scholarly practices in the age of social media. *British Journal of Educational Technology*, 24(3), 392–402.

Grevet, C., Choi, D., Kumar, D., & Gilbert, E. (2014). Overload is overloaded: E-mail in the age of gmail. Proceedings of the 32nd annual ACM conference on Human Factors in computing systems – CHI'14.

Gruber, T. (2014). Academic sell-out: How an obsession with metrics and rankings is damaging academia. *Journal of Marketing for Higher Education*, 24(2), 165–177. doi:10.1080/08841241.2014.970248

Hamilton, M. (2012). *Literacy and the politics of representation*. London: Routledge.

Hamilton, M., & Pitt, K. (2009). Creativity in academic writing. In A. Carter, T. M. Lillis, & S. Parkin (Eds.), *Why writing matters: Issues of accessibility and identity in writing research and pedagogy* (pp. 61–80). Amsterdam: John Benjamins.

Harley, D., Acord, S. K., Earl-Novell, S., Lawrence, S., & Judson King, C. (2010). *Assessing the future landscape of scholarly communication: An exploration of faculty values and needs in seven disciplines*. Retrieved from Center for Research Evaluation (BU), Los Angeles, CA and London https://escholarship.org/uc/item/15x7385g

Hassan, R. (2003). Network time and the new knowledge epoch. *Time & Society*, 12 (2), 225–241.

Heath, S. B. (1983). *Ways with words: Language, life, and work in communities and classrooms*. Cambridge: Cambridge University Press.

Henwood, F., Kennedy, H., & Miller, N. (2001). *Cyborg lives? Women's technobiographies*. York: Raw Nerve Books Ltd.

Hochschild, A. (1997). *The time bind: When work becomes home and home becomes work*. New York: Metropolitan Books.

Holborow, M. (2013). Applied linguistics in the neoliberal university: Ideological keywords and social agency. *Applied Linguistics Review*, 4(2), 229–257. doi:10.1515/applirev-2013-0011

Hyland, K. (2005). Stance and engagement: A model of interaction in academic discourse. *Discourse Studies*, 7(2), 173–191.

Hyland, K. (2012). *Disciplinary identities: Individuality and community in academic discourse*. Cambridge: Cambridge University Press.

Hyland, K. (2015). Genre, discipline and identity. *Journal of English for Academic Purposes*, 19, 32–43.

Iedema, R., & Scheeres, H. (2003). From doing work to talking work: Renegotiating knowing, doing, and identity. *Applied Linguistics*, 24(3), 316–337.

Ingold, T. (2011). *Being alive: Essays on movement, knowledge and description*. London: Taylor & Francis.

Ivanič, R. (1998). *Writing and identity: The discoursal construction of identity in academic writing*. Amsterdam: John Benjamins.

Ivanič, R., Edwards, R., Barton, D., Martin-Jones, M., Fowler, Z., Hughes, B., Mannion, G., Miller, K., & Satchwell, C. (2009). *Improving learning in college: Rethinking literacies across the curriculum*. London: Routledge.

Jaffe, A. (Ed.) (2009). *Stance: Sociolinguistic perspectives*. Oxford: Oxford University Press.

Jarrahi, M., Nelson, S. B., & Thomson, L. (2017). Personal artefact ecologies in the context of mobile knowledge workers. *Computers in Human Behavior, 75*, 469–483.

Jerejian, A. C. M., Reid, C., & Rees, C. S. (2013). The contribution of email volume, email management strategies and propensity to worry in predicting email stress among academics. *Computers in Human Behavior, 29*(3), 991–996. doi:10.1016/j.chb.2012.12.037

Johansson, A., & Vinthagen, S. (2016). Dimensions of everyday resistance: An analytical framework. *Critical Sociology, 42*(3), 417–435.

Johnson, R., Watkinson, A., & Mabe, M. (2018). *The STM report: An overview of scientific and scholarly publishing*. The Hague: International Association of Scientific, Technical and Medical Publishers. Retrieved from www.stm-assoc.org/2018_10_04_STM_Report_2018.pdf

Kalman, J. (1999). *Writing on the plaza*. Cresskill: Hampton Press.

Kalman, J., & Street, B. (2013). *Literacy and numeracy in Latin America*. New York: Routledge.

Karr-Wisniewski, P., & Lu, Y. (2010). When more is too much: Operationalizing technology overload and exploring its impact on knowledge worker productivity. *Computers in Human Behavior, 26*(5), 1061–1072.

Kennedy, H. (2003). Technobiography: Researching lives, online and off. *Biography, 26*(1), 120–139.

Kress, G. (2013). *Multimodality: A social semiotic approach to contemporary communication*. London: Routledge.

Kuteeva, M., & McGrath, L. (2015). The theoretical research article as a reflection of disciplinary practices: The case of pure mathematics. *Applied Linguistics, 36*(2), 215–235. doi:10.1093/applin/amt042

Lakoff, G., & Johnson, M. (1980). *Metaphors we live by*. Chicago and London: University of Chicago Press.

Lambert, C. (2016). *Shadow work: The unpaid, unseen jobs that fill your day*. London: Counterpoint Press.

Lankshear, C., & Knobel, M. (2003). *New literacies: Changing knowledge and classroom learning*. Maidenhead: Open University Press.

Latour, B. (1987). *Science in action: How to follow scientists and engineers through society*. Cambridge, MA: Harvard University Press.

Latour, B. (1999). *Pandora's hope: Essays on the reality of science studies*. Cambridge, MA: Harvard University Press.

Latour, B., & Woolgar, S. (1986). *Laboratory life: The construction of scientific facts* (Second edition). Princeton: Princeton University Press.

Lawn, M., & Grosvenor, I. (Eds.) (2005). *Materialities of schooling: Design, technology, objects, routines*. Oxford: Symposium Books.

Lea, M. R., & Stierer, B. (2009). Lecturers' everyday writing as professional practice in the university as workplace: New insights into academic identities. *Studies in Higher Education, 34*(4), 417–428.

Lea, M. R., & Stierer, B. (2011). Changing academic identities in changing academic workplaces: Learning from academics' everyday professional writing practices. *Teaching in Higher Education, 16*(6), 605–616.

Lea, M. R., & Street, B. V. (1998). Student writing in higher education: An academic literacies approach. *Studies in Higher Education, 23*(2), 157–172.

Lea, M. R., & Street, B. V. (2006). The academic literacies model: Theory and applications. *Theory into Practice, 45*(4), 368–377.

Lefebvre, H. (1991). *The production of space.* Oxford: Blackwell.

Lemke, J. L. (2000). Across the scales of time: Artifacts, activities, and meanings in ecosocial systems. *Mind, Culture, and Activity,* 7(4), 273–290.

Leon, K., & Pigg, S. (2011). Graduate students professionalizing in digital time/space: A view from "down below". *Computers and Composition,* 28(1), 3–13.

Liao, T. F., Beckman, J., Marzolph, E., Riederer, C., Sayler, J., & Schmelkin, L. (2013). The social definition of time for university students. *Time & Society,* 22(1), 119–151.

Lillis, T., & Curry, M. J. (2006). Professional academic writing by multilingual scholars: Interactions with literacy brokers in the production of English-medium texts. *Written Communication,* 23(1), 3–35.

Lillis, T. M., & Curry, M. J. (2010). *Academic writing in a global context: The politics and practices of publishing in English.* London: Routledge.

Lillis, T. M., & Maybin, J. (Eds) (2017). The dynamics of textual trajectories in professional and workplace practice. *Text and Talk,* 37(4), 409–414.

Lillis, T. M., & Scott, M. (2007). Defining academic literacies research: Issues of epistemology, ideology and strategy. *Journal of Applied Linguistics,* 4(1), 5–32.

Lingard, B., & Thompson, G. (2017). Doing time in the sociology of education. *British Journal of Sociology of Education,* 38(1), 1–12. doi:10.1080/01425692.2016.1260854

Luff, P., Hindmarsh, J., & Heath, C. (2000). *Workplace studies: Recovering work practice and informing system design.* Cambridge: Cambridge University Press.

Lupton, D. (2013, September 16). Academics online: What are the risks? Retrieved from https://simplysociology.wordpress.com/2013/09/16/academics-online-what-a re-the-risks/

Lupton, D. (2014). *"Feeling better connected": Academics' use of social media.* Canberra: News & Media Research Centre, University of Canberra.

Massey, D. (1994). *Space, place and gender.* Cambridge: Polity Press.

Mautner, G. (2005). The entrepreneurial university. *Critical Discourse Studies,* 2(2), 95–120. doi:10.1080/17405900500283540

Mautner, G. (2010). *Language and the market society.* London: Routledge.

May, J., & Thrift, N. (Eds.) (2003). *Timespace: Geographies of temporality.* Abingdon: Routledge.

Maybin, J., & Tusting, K. (2011). Linguistic ethnography. In J. Simpson (Ed.), *Routledge handbook of applied linguistics* (pp. 515–528). London: Routledge.

Mayr, A. (2008). Discourses of higher education: Enterprise and institutional change in the university. In A. Mayr (Ed.), *Language and power: An introduction to institutional discourse* (pp. 26–45). London: Continuum.

McCarty, R., & Swales, J. M. (2017). Technological change and generic effects in a university Herbarium: A textography revisited. *Discourse Studies,* 19(5), 561–580.

McCulloch, S. (2017). Hobson's choice: The effects of research evaluation on academics' writing practices in England. *Aslib Journal of Information Management,* 69 (5), 503–515.

McCulloch, S., Tusting, K., & Hamilton, M. (2017). The role of networked learning in academics' writing. *Research in Learning Technology,* 25. doi:10.25304/rlt.v25.1958

McGrath, L., & Kaufhold, K. (2016). English for specific purposes and academic literacies: Eclecticism in academic writing pedagogy. *Teaching in Higher Education,* 21 (8), 933–947.

McGrath, L., & Kuteeva, M. (2012). Stance and engagement in pure mathematics research articles: Linking discourse features to disciplinary practices. *English for Specific Purposes,* 31(3), 161–173.

Menzies, H., & Newson, J. (2007). No time to think: Academics' life in the globally wired university. *Time & Society*, 16(1), 83–98.

Merchant, G. (2009). Web 2.0, new literacies, and the idea of learning through participation. *English Teaching: Practice and Critique*, 8(3), 8–20.

Miller, C. R. (1984). Genre as social action. *Quarterly Journal of Speech*, 70(2), 151–167.

Mingers, J., & Willmott, H. (2012). Taylorizing business school research: On the "one best way" performative effects of journal ranking lists. *Human Relations*, 66(8), 1051–1073. doi:10.1177/0018726712467048

Misra, J., Lundquist, J. H., & Templer, A. (2012). Gender, work time, and care responsibilities among faculty. *Sociological Forum*, 27(2), 300–323.

Morrish, L. (2018). A short commercial break, on *Academic irregularities: Critical university studies, discourse and managerialism*. Retrieved from https://academicirre gularities.wordpress.com/2018/10/06/a-short-commercial-break/

Müller, R. (2014). Racing for what? Anticipation and acceleration in the work and career practices of academic life science postdocs. *Forum: Qualitative Social Research*, 15(3). doi:10.17169/fqs-15.3.2245

Murray, R. (2015). *Writing in social spaces: A social processes approach to academic writing*. London: Routledge.

Murray, R., & Newton, M. (2009). Writing retreat as structured intervention: Margin or mainstream? *Higher Education Research & Development*, 28(5), 541–553.

Myers, G. (1990). *Writing biology: Texts in the social construction of scientific knowledge* (Vol. 8). Madison: University of Wisconsin Press.

Myers, G. (2010). *The discourse of blogs and wikis*. London: Continuum.

Naidoo, R., & Williams, J. (2015). The neoliberal regime in English higher education: Charters, consumers and the erosion of the public good. *Critical Studies in Education*, 56(2), 208–223.

Nespor, J. (2007). Curriculum charts and time in undergraduate education. *British Journal of Sociology of Education*, 28(6), 753–766.

Nespor, J. (2014). *Knowledge in motion: Space, time and curriculum in undergraduate physics and management*. London: Routledge.

Neumann, A. (2009) *Professing to learn: Creating tenured lives and careers in the American research university*. Baltimore: The Johns Hopkins University.

Nygaard, L. P. (2017). Publishing and perishing: An academic literacies framework for investigating research productivity. *Studies in Higher Education*, 42(3), 519–532. doi:10.1080/03075079.2015.1058351

Obeng-Denteh, W., & Amoah-Mensah, J. (2011). Pure mathematicians' and applied mathematicians' saga: But one family! A mathematical panacea. *Continental Journal of Education Research*, 4(2), 1–10.

O'Carroll, A. (2008). Fuzzy holes and intangible time: Time in a knowledge industry. *Time & Society*, 17(2–3), 179–193. doi:10.1177/0961463X08093421

Olssen, M., & Peters, M. A. (2005). Neoliberalism, higher education and the knowledge economy: From the free market to knowledge capitalism. *Journal of Education Policy*, 20(3), 313–345. doi:10.1080/02680930500108718

O'Reilly, T. (2005, July 27). What is Web 2.0? Retrieved from http://oreilly.com/web2/a rchive/what-is-web-20.html

Orlikowski, W. J. (2007). Sociomaterial practices: Exploring technology at work. *Organization Studies*, 28(9), 1435–1448.

Oztok, M., Wilton, L., Lee, K., Wilton, L., Zingaro, D., MacKinnon, K., … Hewitt, J. (2014). Polysynchronous: Dialogic construction of time in online learning. *E-Learning and Digital Media*, 11(2), 154–161. doi:10.2304/elea.2014.11.2.154

Page, R., Barton, D., Unger, J. W., & Zappavigna, M. (2014). *Researching language and social media: A student guide.* London and New York: Routledge.

Paltridge, B., Starfield, S., & Tardy, C. (2016). *Ethnographic perspectives on academic writing.* Oxford: Oxford University Press.

Pardoe, S. (2000). Respect and the pursuit of "symmetry" in researching literacy and student writing. In D. Barton, M. Hamilton, & R. Ivanič (Eds.), *Situated literacies: Reading and writing in context* (pp. 149–166). London: Routledge.

Park, J. H., & De Costa, P. (2015). Reframing graduate student writing strategies from an activity theory perspective. *Language and Sociocultural Theory*, 2(1), 25–50.

Pels, D. (2003). Unhastening science. *European Journal of Social Theory*, 6(2), 209–231.

Pells, R. (2018) Gender pay gap: How much less are women paid at your university? *Times Higher Education*, April 6.

Prior, P. A. (1998). *Writing/disciplinarity: A sociohistoric account of literate activity in the academy.* Mahwah: Lawrence Erlbaum.

Prior, P., & Shipka, J. (2003). Chronotopic lamination: Tracing the contours of literate activity. In C. Bazerman & D. R. Russell (Eds.), *Writing selves, writing societies: Research from activity perspectives* (pp. 180–238). Fort Collins: WAC Clearinghouse and Mind, Culture, and Activity.

Probert, B. (2005). "I just couldn't fit it in": Gender and unequal outcomes in academic careers. *Gender, Work & Organization*, 12(1), 50–72.

Radice, H. (2013). How we got here: UK higher education under neoliberalism. *ACME: An International E-Journal for Critical Geographies*, 12(3), 407–418.

REF (2015a). *Research excellence framework 2014: Overview report by main panel C and sub-panels 16 to 26.* Retrieved from www.ref.ac.uk/2014/media/ref/content/expa nel/member/Main%20Panel%20C%20overview%20report.pdf

REF (2015b). *Research excellence framework 2014: Overview report by main panel B and sub-panels 7 to 15.* Retrieved from www.ref.ac.uk/2014/media/ref/content/expa nel/member/Main%20Panel%20B%20overview%20report.pdf

Robertson, S. L. (2014). Corporatisation, competitiveness, commercialisation: New logics in the globalising of UK higher education. In E. Hartmann (Ed.), *The internationalisation of higher education* (pp. 31–44). Abingdon and New York: Routledge.

Russell, D. (2002). *Writing in the academic disciplines.* Carbondale and Edwardsville: S. Illinois University Press.

Ryberg, T., Davidsen, J., & Hodgson, V. (2017). Understanding nomadic collaborative learning groups. *British Journal of Educational Technology*, 49(2), 235–247. doi:10.1111/bjet.12584

Satchwell, C., Barton, D., & Hamilton, M. (2013). Crossing boundaries: Digital and non-digital literacy practices in formal and informal contexts in further and higher education. In R. Goodfellow & M. R. Lea (Eds.), *Literacy in the digital university: Critical perspectives on learning, scholarship, and technology* (pp. 42–55). London and New York: Routledge.

Scollon, R. (2002). *Mediated discourse: The nexus of practice.* London: Routledge.

Scott, J. C. (1990). *Domination and the arts of resistance: Hidden transcripts.* New Haven and London: Yale University Press.

Scribner, S., & Cole, M. (1981). *The psychology of literacy.* Cambridge, MA and London: Harvard University Press.

Shattock, M. (2014). Can we still speak of there being an academic profession? *History of Education*, 43(6), 727–739. doi:10.1080/0046760X.2014.964008

Shepherd, S. (2018). Managerialism: An ideal type. *Studies in Higher Education*, 43(9), 1668–1678. doi:10.1080/03075079.2017.1281239

Shove, E., Pantzar, M., & Watson, M. (2012). *The dynamics of social practice: Everyday life and how it changes.* London: Sage.

Smith, S. (2015). Multiple temporalities of knowing in academic research. *Social Science Information,* 54(2), 149–176.

Snyder, I. (Ed.) (2002). *Silicon literacies: Communication, innovation and education in the electronic age.* London: Routledge.

Southerton, D. (2003). "Squeezing time": Allocating practices, coordinating networks and scheduling society. *Time & Society,* 12(1), 5–25.

Star, S. L., & Griesemer, J. R. (1989). Institutional ecology, "translations" and boundary objects: Amateurs and professionals in Berkeley's Museum of Vertebrate Zoology, 1907–1939. *Social Studies of Science,* 19(3), 387–420. doi:10.1177/030631289019003001

Star, S. L., & Strauss, A. (1999). Layers of silence, arenas of voice: The ecology of visible and invisible work. *Computer Supported Cooperative Work (CSCW),* 8(1–2), 9–30.

Stern, N. (2016). *Building on success and learning from experience: An independent review of the Research Excellence Framework.* London: Department for Business, Energy and Industrial Strategy. Retrieved from https://assets.publishing.service.gov.uk/government/uploads/system/uploads/attachment_data/file/541338/ind-16-9-ref-stern-review.pdf

Strathern, M. (2000). *Audit cultures: Anthropological studies in accountability, ethics and the academy.* London and New York: Routledge.

Street, B. (1984). *Literacy in theory and practice.* Cambridge: Cambridge University Press.

Suchman, L. (2007). *Human-machine reconfigurations: Plans and situated actions.* Cambridge: Cambridge University Press.

Sum, N. L., & Jessop, B. J. (2013). Competitiveness, the knowledge-based economy and higher education. *Journal of the Knowledge Economy,* 4(24), 24–44. doi:10.1007/s13132–012–0121–8

Swales, J. M. (1990). *Genre analysis: English in academic and research settings.* Cambridge: Cambridge University Press.

Swales, J. M. (1998). *Other floors, other voices: A textography of a small university building.* Hillsdale: Lawrence Erlbaum Associates.

Swales, J. (2004). *Research genres: Explorations and applications.* Cambridge: Cambridge University Press.

Swales, J. M. (2018). *Other floors, other voices: A textography of a small university building: 20th anniversary edition.* Ann Arbor: University of Michigan Press.

Taberner, A. M. (2018). The marketisation of the English higher education sector and its impact on academic staff and the nature of their work. *International Journal of Organizational Analysis,* 26(1), 129–152. doi:10.1108/IJOA-07-2017-1198

Taylor, S., & Spicer, A. (2007). Time for space: A narrative review of research on organizational spaces. *International Journal of Management Reviews,* 9(4), 325–346.

Temple, P. (Ed.) (2014). *The physical university: Contours of space and place in higher education.* Abingdon: Routledge.

Temple, P., & Barnett, R. (2007). Higher education space: Future directions. *Planning for Higher Education,* 36(1), 5–15.

Terras, M. (2012, April 3). Is blogging and tweeting about research papers worth it? The verdict. Retrieved from http://melissaterras.blogspot.co.uk/2012/04/is-blogging-and-tweeting-about-research.html

Tight, M. (Ed.) (2000). *Academic work and life: What it is to be an academic, and how this is changing.* New York: JAI Press.

Tourish, D., & Willmott, H. (2015). In defiance of folly: Journal rankings, mindless measures and the ABS Guide. *Critical Perspectives on Accounting*, 26, 37–46. doi:10.1016/j.cpa.2014.02.004

Trowler, P. (2014). Depicting and researching disciplines: Strong and moderate essentialist approaches. *Studies in Higher Education*, 39(10), 1720–1731.

Trowler, P., Saunders, M., & Bamber, V. (2012). *Tribes and territories in the 21st century: Rethinking the significance of disciplines in higher education*. London: Routledge.

Tuck, J. (2018a). *Academics engaging with student writing: Working at the higher education textface*. Abingdon: Routledge.

Tuck, J. (2018b). "I'm nobody's Mum in this university": The gendering of work around student writing in UK higher education. *Journal of English for Academic Purposes*, 32, 32–41. doi:10.1016/j.jeap.2018.03.006

Tusting, K. (2012). Learning accountability literacies in educational workplaces: Situated learning and processes of commodification. *Language and Education*, 26(2), 121–138.

Tusting, K. (2013). Literacy studies as linguistic ethnography (Working paper no. 105). Working papers in urban language and literacies. London. Retrieved from https://core.ac.uk/download/pdf/16285101.pdf

Tusting, K. (2018). The genre regime of research evaluation: Contradictory systems of value around academics' writing. *Language and Education* (early online publication).

Tusting, K., Wilson, A., & Ivanič, R. (2000). New literacy studies at the interchange. In D. Barton, M. Hamilton, & R. Ivanič (Eds.), *Situated literacies: Reading and writing in context* (pp. 210–218). London: Routledge.

UCU (University and College Union) (2015). *Work-related wellbeing in UK higher education – 2014*. London: University and College Union. Retrieved from http://hdl.handle.net/10547/622171

UCU (University and College Union) (2016). *Precarious work in higher education: A snapshot of insecure contracts and institutional attitudes*. London: University and College Union. Retrieved from www.ucu.org.uk/media/7995/Precarious-work-in-higher-education-a-snapshot-of-insecure-contracts-and-institutional-attitudes-Apr-16/pdf/ucu_precariouscontract_hereport_apr16.pdf

Van Marrewijk, A., & Yanow, D. (Eds.) (2010). *Organizational spaces: Rematerializing the workaday world*. Cheltenham: Edward Elgar Publishing.

Veletsianos, G. (2012). Higher education scholars' participation and practices on twitter. *Journal of Computer Assisted Learning*, 28(4), 336–349.

Wargo, J. M., & De Costa, P. I. (2017). Tracing academic literacies across contemporary literacy sponsorscapes: Mobilities, ideologies, identities, and technologies. *London Review of Education*, 15(1), 101–114.

Watermeyer, R. (2016). Impact in the REF: Issues and obstacles. *Studies in Higher Education*, 41(2), 199–214. doi:10.1080/03075079.2014.915303

Weller, M. (2011). *The digital scholar: How technology is transforming scholarly practice*. London: Bloomsbury.

Whittaker, S., & Sidner, C. (1996). Email overload: Exploring personal information management of email. *Proceedings of CHI 96 Conference on Human Factors in Computing Systems* (pp. 276–283). New York: ACM.

Widerberg, K. (2006). Embodying modern times: Investigating tiredness. *Time & Society*, 15(1), 105–120.

Wilkins, S., & Huisman, J. (2012). The international branch campus as transnational strategy in higher education. *Higher Education*, 64(5), 627–645. doi:10.1007/s10734-012-9516-5

Willmott, H. (2011). Journal list fetishism and the perversion of scholarship: Reactivity and the ABS list. *Organization*, 18(4), 429–442. doi:10.1177/1350508411403532

Yates, J., & Orlikowski, W. (1992). Genres of organizational communication: A structurational approach to studying communication and media. *Academy of Management Review*, 17(22), 299–326.

Ylijoki, O.-H., & Mäntylä, H. (2003). Conflicting time perspectives in academic work. *Time & Society*, 12(1), 55–78.

# INDEX

Note: page references in *italics* indicate figures; **bold** indicates tables.

academia.edu 98
academic networking sites 9, 92, 93, 97, 98
academic writing practices 1–2, 7–8; data analysis 24–26, *25*; future research 146–148; implications of findings on 143–146; research design 16–17; research events 26; research methodology 17–24, 147; research on 5–7
accountability 3, 36–37, 43, 57, 63, 106, 136–137, 147
administrative work 34, 36–37, 55–56, 60, 66, 113–117, 132, 138–139, 142, 144–145
Adobe Connect 38
affect 79, 80, 82, 83–84, 85
Ainsworth, S. 51
Altmetric 96
anxiety 137, 140; *see also* stress
application forms 31
appraisal 29, 96, 136
apprenticeship 121–124
archives 50
assemblages 13
assessment/evaluation 4, 5, 9, 16, 25, 34, 36, 63, 68, 77, 81, 96, 136, 138
ATLAS.ti 24
audience 3, 9, 13, 64, 80, 92, 97–101, 103, 105, 136, 138, 142, 146, 148
authority 14

auto-ethnography 8, 19, 26
autonomy 39–40, 45, 132, 135–136, 140

Barton, D. 11, 12, 13, 15, 20
Bazerman, C. 6, 16
Bhatia, V. K. 65
Bhatt, I. 21, 81
blackboards 75–76
blogs 32, 33, 93–95, 98–104
Borgman, C. L. 7
boundaries 59–61, 81, 95, 135–136; *see also* time blocking
Brandt, D. 12, 111

cafés 47, 49, 50
Camtasia 21–22, *22*
career progression 4, 10, 30, 43, 53, 69–70, 78, 98, 120, 140
challenges 8, 46, 53, 58, 61, 100–105, 111, 120, 136, 148
change 41, 139, 147
Chartered Association of Business Schools, *ABS Journal Guide* 67–68
China 148
choice 45, 49, 54; *see also* autonomy
cloud storage 24
coding 24, *25*
collaboration 9–10, 28, 29–30, 31, 34, 106–119; administrative writing 113–117; futures of 138–139; learning through 123–124, 131, 133; in research

writing 107–110; service relations
117–118; teaching 110–113
colleagues, academic 2, 3, 5, 22, 24, 116,
119, 122; *see also* collaboration
colleagues, administrative 22, 24, 49, 60,
81–82, 94, 107, 114, 116–117, 138
computer use 33, 36; *see also* laptop use
conference papers 72, 85, 107
conferences 110
consultancy work 16, 69–70, 129
contracts, work 39–40, 53
corporatisation 3–4, 132, 140
course descriptions 31, 114–115
co-writers 21, 123; *see also* collaboration
creative thinking/writing 3, 52, 56, 61,
112, 140–141, 142, 145, 148
critical thinking 108, 141
Curry, M. J. 6, 11

data tools/resources 80–81
Davidsen, J. 108
day-in-the-life interviews 20–21
De Costa, P. I. 112
deadlines 53, 55
departments 2, 4, 5–6, 10, 16–18, 22, 24,
64, 96, 133, 138, 139, 144; *see also*
head of departments
diaries 130
digital cameras 82
digital devices 37, 49, 57–58, 81, 86, 130;
*see also* smartphone use; tablet use
digital platforms 107–108
digital scholarship 92
digital technology 5–6, 7, 56–57,
79–80, 82–83, 108, 131,
137–138, 141
digitisation 106, 108
disciplines 18, 63–65
distance teaching 38
division of labour 25, 94, 113
drafting 30, 36, 40–41, 43, 49, 89, 108,
113, 116, 126
Dropbox 82, 84

edited collections 76, 125
Edwards, R. 14
email 27–37, 39–43, 57–58, 61,
85–91, 101, 108, 116–117, 130,
138, 139, 144
engineering 18, 52
English language 6, 40, 106, 147, 148
equality 48–49, 145, 147
ethics 21–22
ethnography 6, 8, 12, 13, 17, 20, 21, 53,
137; auto-ethnography 8, 19, 26

evaluation/assessment 4, 5, 9, 16, 25, 34,
36, 63, 68, 77, 81, 96, 136, 138
exams (writing) 34, 128

Facebook 93–95, 97, 99, 102, 110
face-to-face meetings 30, 35, 88, 108, 119,
137–138, 144
family 35, 40, 41, 53, 145
feedback to students 82, 111–113,
121–122
Fenwick, T. 14
file-sharing software 108
finishing, importance of 43
Fraiberg, S. 7
funding 4, 28, 31, 32, 39, 40, 42, 71–72;
*see also* grant applications; research
proposals

gender pay gap 145
genres 63, 65–67, 132, 141, 144
Goodfellow, R. 7
Google 40
Google Drive 28
Google Scholar 96, 97
Gornall, L. 130
Gourlay, L. 7, 57
GradeMark 112
grant applications 32, 71–72, 86, 102,
107, 125; *see also* funding; research
proposals
Gruber, T. 71

Hamilton, M. 7, 11, 15, 20, 78, 121
handwriting 35, 82
hard copies *see* pen and paper
harriedness 61
Hassan, R. 57
head of departments 22, 36, 55, 88,
96–98, 102, 113–114, 118, 123,
128–129; *see also* leadership
higher education *see* universities
history 7, 9, 18, 49, 55, 56, 64–65, 67,
77–78, 95, 98, 100, 128; knowledge
valued in 71–74
Hochschild, A. 52
Hodgson, V. 108
home, working from 27–28, 30–31, 38,
41, 43, 47, 60, 82–83, 135–136, 140;
*see also* family; offices
Hyland, K. 18

identity 3, 14, 105, 141–142
impact 4, 68–70
industrial action (2018) x
industry 3, 39, 51, 52, 127, 135

institutional repositories 92
interdisciplinary work 24, 71–73, 77, 137
international academia 106, 147, 148
international teaching 42
internationalisation 106
Internet writing *see* bogs, social media
interruptions 31, 35, 47–49, 54, 57–59, 61, 62, 90, 119, 135, 143
interviews 19–21; day-in-the-life 20–21; techno-biographical 19–20; walk-along 19
Ivanič, R. 6, 12, 14, 15, 20, 67, 81

Jaffe, A. 83
Jarrahi, M. 86
Je-S 28
Johnson, R. 87
journal articles 5, 28, 34, 35, 38, 39, 41, 53–54, 66–70, 72, 76, 77, 137, 141; *see also* peer review; reviewing for journals
Judson King, C. 71

Keates, J. 7
Kennedy, H. 19–20
knowledge 2–3, 16, 54, 57, 63, 108, 141–142, 148; valued in history 71–74; valued in marketing 67–71; valued in maths 74–77
Kuteeva, M. 18, 76, 77

Lakoff, G. 87
Lambert, C. 86
laptop use 28, 29–30, 31, 38, 41, 50
LaTeX 28, 74, 82, 124
Latour, B. 14
Lawrence, S. 71
Lea, M. R. 6, 11
leadership, writing for 128–129; *see also* head of departments
league tables 4, 96, 115, 136
learning 10, 120–133; career beginnings 121–122; by doing 126–127; futures of 138–139; implications for 145–146; meta-logistical and organisational writing 129–130; peer review 124–125; social media and new technologies 131; through apprenticeship, collaboration, and networking 123–124; using models 125–126; to write for leadership and management 128–129; to write for teaching 127–128; *see also* professional development
lecture slides and notes 33, 66, 75, 85
Lefebvre, H. 46, 53
libraries 47, 50, 80

Lillis, T. 6, 11
LinkedIn 94, 97, 109
literacy events 11–12
literacy practices 11–12, 20
literacy studies 11–16, 20

management 3–4; implications of research for 144–145; learning to write for 128–129; *see also* heads of department
managerialism 1, 43, 57, 63, 106, 136–137
Mäntylä, H. 52
marketing 9, 18, 34–35, 37–43, 47, 49, 58–59, 64–65, 76–78, 82, 90, 94, 97, 100, 108, 121–124, 126–129, 131; knowledge valued in 67–71
marketisation x, 57, 71, 115, 117
marking 43, 56, 82, 111–112
Massey, D. 46
maths 9, 18, 24, 27–30, 33, 47, 49, 51, 54, 55, 60–61, 64–65, 67, 82, 93, 96, 109, 118, 123–125, 128, 130, 131; knowledge valued in 74–77
May, J. 46, 58
McCulloch, S. 68, 121
McGrath, L. 18, 76, 77
media engagement *see* public engagement; social media
meetings 29–30, 35, 36, 53, 84; face-to-face 30, 35, 88, 108, 119, 137–138, 144
mentoring 123; *see also* apprenticeship
Menzies, H. 57, 108
Merchant, G. 93
Messenger 94
meta-logistics 129–130
methods 15, 17, 19, 21, 26, 64, 80, 128
Mingers, J. 71
modelling 121–122, 125–126
monographs 5, 69, 71, 141
Müller, R. 53
multitasking 29–30
Murray, Rowena 144

National Student Survey (NSS) 136
Nelson, S. B. 86
neoliberalism 3, 57, 118
Nespor, J. 54–55
networks 1, 13, 110, 123–124, 133
Neumann, A. 130
Newson, J. 57, 108
notebooks 35, 42
notes for self 130

O'Carroll, A. 52, 54, 88
offices 29, 31, 32, 37–38, 47–48, *48*, *50*, 50–51, 60; *see also* travelling, writing while; working from home
O'Reilly, T. 93
organisational writing 129–130
Orlikowski, W. J. 65
overload 41, 44, 57, 87, 89, 90, 116, 132, 139; *see also* workload
Oztok, M. 58

Page, R. 20
Pardoe, S. 15
peer review 5, 69, 77–78, 124–125, 131–132
Pels, D. 57
pen and paper 28, 29, 30, 34, 35, 130
PhD students 29–30, 37–38, 98, 128
PhD supervision 27–28
PhD supervisors 109, 121–122
PhD/doctoral studies 42, 113, 121–122, 132–133
Post-It notes 130
power relationships 15–16, 46
PowerPoint 32, 33, 41, 66, 75, 84–85, 137–138
pressure 139–141
Prezi 85
printers 33–34
prioritising tasks 30, 40, 41, 43, 53, 55, 69, 101, 114, 137, 147
probation 38, 39
professional development 8, 10, 26, 81, 120, 132, 134, 143, 145–146; *see also* learning
proofreading 121
public engagement 92, 95, 100, 117, 118

qualitative data analysis 8, 66
Quality Assurance Agency (QAA) 36, 115
quality processes 4, 115

rankings 4, 67–68, 71
reactivity 37–38
reading 41
REF (Research Excellence Framework) 4–5, 55, 67–68, 70–72, 74, 77, 78, 136–137, 140, 145; documentation 5, 32, 33, 60, 126
reference letters 66
reference managers (Endnote, Mendeley) 67, 73
report writing 34, 36–37
Research Assessment Exercise (RAE) 4

research proposals 28, 39, 66, 123, 125, 132; *see also* funding; grant applications
ResearchGate 97, 98
research-intensive universities 4, 27–33, 34–37, 38–39, 40–41, 125–126, 146–147
research-related writing 31, 35, 36, 37, 38, 39, 41, 55, 56, 66, 142, 145; sharing in 107–110; teaching and 111
reviewing for journals 43
revising writing 36, 41, 66
rhythm 27, 28–30, 35, 38–39, 53, 135
risk-taking 68, 140
routines 32, 61
Ryberg, T. 108

Salisbury, J. 130
Scollon, R. 1, 12
Scott, J. 139–140
screen-in-screen recording 21–22, *22*
self-blame 143
self-promotion 93, 104
service relations 66, 117–118
Shattock, M. 4
"Shut up and Write Tuesdays" (@SUWTues) 143–144
Sidner, C. 89–90
Skype 82, 84, 108
small tasks, clearing away 27–28
smartphone use 5, 9, 28, 79, 81, 83, 95; *see also* digital devices
Smith, S. 53
social media 9, 20, 92–105, 109–110, 131, 138, 143–144; advantages and possibilities of 98–100; attitudes to 97–98; challenges associated with 100–105; practices on different platforms 93–96; professional identity and future implications 105; *see also* Facebook; LinkedIn; Twitter
social scholarship 109
social sciences 18, 64, 73, 82, 94, 127, 129
socio-material theory 2, 11–17, 46, 134, 135
Southerton, D. 61
space of work 46–52, *48*, *50*, *51*, 135–136; strategies 58–61, 143–144; *see also* offices; working from home
spreadsheets 49
stance-taking 83–91
Stierer, B. 6, 11
Street, B. 11, 12, 15
stress 57, 80, 87, 90, 130, 139–141
student handbooks 35, 74–75, 115

student record systems 7, 113
students 3, 34, 37, 38, 58, 94, 95,
    111–112, 114; *see also* feedback to
    students; marking; PhD students;
    teaching
support: from colleagues 39–40; from
    universities 145, 148–149
Swales, J. 5–6, 16, 65

Taberner, A. M. 147
tablet use 58, 86, 88; *see also* digital
    devices
teaching 29–30, 32–34, 38–39, 42, 54–55,
    66, 75, 106, 136; collaboration
    110–113; learning to write for 127–128
teaching materials 31, 142; *see also*
    lecture notes and slides; student
    handbooks
teaching-intensive universities 33–34,
    37–38, 42–43, 51, 127–128, 146–147
technobiography 19–20
technology 9, 28, 31, 40, 79–91, 83–84;
    *see also* digital technology
telephones 107
template documents 36, 37, 38,
    114, 115
textbooks 69
theses 10, 59, 113, 120, 122
Thomson, L. 86
Thrift, N. 46, 58
time 41–42, 52–58, 108, 135–136;
    strategies 58–61, 89, 143–144
time blocking 36, 56, 58–59, 135, 144; *see
    also* boundaries
time/space theory 45–46
to-do lists 97, 130, 141
Tourish, D. 71
training 12, 102, 123, 129–132, 138, 139,
    145; *see also* learning; professional
    development
transcriptions 31
travelling, writing while 28, 47, 49
trolling 103
Trowler, P. 18
Turnitin 111, 112

Tusting, K. 11, 78, 121
Twitter 33, 65, 93–95, 97, 99–105, 110,
    143–144

Unger, J. W. 20
universities 1–5, 17–18, 46, 49, 57, 62,
    141, 149; corporatisation of 3–4, 132,
    140; management, implications of
    research for 144–145; marketisation of
    x, 57, 71, 115, 117; support from 145,
    148–149; *see also* research-intensive
    universities; teaching-intensive
    universities
university buildings 29, 30, 47, 51, *51*; *see
    also* libraries; offices

videography 21–22, *22*, **23**, 90
virtual learning environments (VLE)
    (Moodle, Blackboards) 31, 32, 33, 38,
    39, 58, 75, 79, 80–82, 137

walk-along interviews 19
Wargo, J. M. 112
Weller, M. 7, 92
WhatsApp 104
Whittaker, S. 89–90
Widerberg, K. 52
Willmott, H. 71
women 147
word processing 82, 84, 85
WordPress 103
working from home 27–28, 30–31, 38, 41,
    43, 47, 60, 82–83, 135–136, 140
working hours 32, 41, 42, 58, 59–60, 145
work–life balance 61, 139
workloads 31, 33, 66, 80, 94–95, 102,
    111, 113–114, 116–117, 119, 130, 135,
    138–139, 143
writing retreats 144
Wunderlist 130

Yates, J. 65
Ylijoki, O.-H. 52

Zappavigna, M. 20

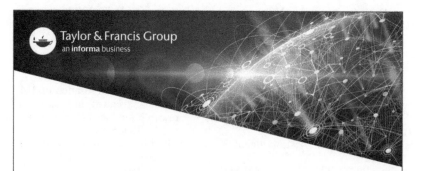